The Norwegian-American Historical Association
ARTHUR O. DAVIDSON, *president*

Board of Publications

KENNETH O. BJORK, *editor*. ARLOW W. ANDERSEN, C. A. CLAUSEN,
CARL H. CHRISLOCK, ERIK J. FRIIS, CLARENCE A. GLASRUD,
EINAR HAUGEN, ODD S. LOVOLL, PETER A. MUNCH,
CARLTON C. QUALEY

Waldemar Ager

TOPICAL STUDIES • VOLUME 2

CULTURAL PLURALISM
versus ASSIMILATION

The Views of Waldemar Ager

Edited by ODD S. LOVOLL

Introduction by Carl H. Chrislock

1977

The Norwegian-American Historical Association

NORTHFIELD, MINNESOTA

Copyright © 1977 by the Norwegian-American Historical Association

87732:58

Printed in the United States of America at the
North Central Publishing Company, St. Paul

Preface

THE Norwegian Society of America (Det Norske Selskap), founded in 1903, ceases to exist as an independent organization with the appearance of the present publication, which contains articles from its official organ, *Kvartalskrift* (Quarterly), published from 1905 to 1922. In this magazine Waldemar Ager, its editor, argued for a pluralistic view of American life. His contentions were opposed by Norwegian Americans who accepted the inevitability of a rapid and total assimilation of all ethnic groups into American society. Their exchange of opinions gives a vivid impression of the debate, as well as the agony, experienced by one immigrant group in trying to define its position in the New World.

In 1974, the board of trustees and the officers of the Society resolved to translate and publish a group of essays from *Kvartalskrift*. Odd S. Lovoll, the Society's president, and Carl H. Chrislock, a member of its board, selected the articles. They limited their choices to essays dealing with the issues of cultural pluralism and assimilation. The selections were subsequently translated by Sigvald Stoylen, a retired high-school teacher of English and treasurer of the Society; Ben R. Eggan, a long-time member of the Society's board and a teacher of Norwegian;

Leif E. Hansen, head of Augsburg College's department of Norwegian and the Society's secretary; Odd S. Lovoll, assistant professor of Norwegian and immigration history in St. Olaf College; Liv Dahl, who has been active in Norwegian-American affairs and in the Camp Norway language program; and Carl H. Chrislock, professor of history in Augsburg College.

Professor Chrislock presents a broad introduction to the essays and, in so doing, provides within the context of American history a penetrating interpretation of the Norwegian-American experience. Focusing on organizational drives after the turn of the century, he traces the background and growth of a Norwegian subculture, delineates its shifting fortunes, and indicates the forces affecting Norwegian-American ethnicity. Kenneth Smemo, professor of history and director of Scandinavian studies in Moorhead State University, writes succinctly about Waldemar Ager and his role in the immigrant community.

Ralph L. Henry, professor emeritus of English in Carleton College, has assisted in all phases of the editing process. All explanatory notes have been added by the editor and formulated to serve the needs of a general reading public as well as of students at the secondary level.

We present these essays in the hope that they will stimulate fruitful thinking about the character of American society, past and present, and that they may stand as a monument to the work and mission of the Norwegian Society and to the men and women who participated in its program. By action of its members, the Society in 1976 merged with the Norwegian-American Historical Association, and its name will be perpetuated in a special fund created for the purpose of promoting interest among young people in the Norwegian-American heritage.

ODD S. LOVOLL

St. Olaf College

Foreword

As DR. ODD S. LOVOLL explains in his preface, the Norwegian Society of America (Det Norske Selskap), in terminating its separate existence, merged with the Norwegian-American Historical Association in 1976, also transferring its funds to the younger organization. In preparing for the merger, the officers of the Society resolved to publish, on their own initiative, a volume of essays written by or in response to the views of Waldemar Ager, long-time editor of their periodical, *Kvartalskrift* (Quarterly). The Association's executive board in turn voted unanimously in favor of distributing copies of the Socity's book to the members of the NAHA.

After carefully examining the Society's manuscript, ably edited by Dr. Lovoll, the Association's board of publications approved my recommendation that it be published by the Association. Their decision was a happy one, as the contemplated book met the standards set earlier for our Topical Studies: It deals with one of the most vital themes in American history; Ager's views on the subject are highly controversial; and the book is short in length. *Cultural Pluralism versus Assimilation: The Views of Waldemar Ager* thus becomes the second volume in our Topical Studies series. We hope that it also will serve as a fitting memorial to the work of the Norwegian Society of America.

K.O.B.

Contents

PREFACE   *page* v

FOREWORD   *page* vii

I   INTRODUCTION: THE HISTORICAL CONTEXT by CARL H. CHRISLOCK . *page* 3

II   OUR CULTURAL STAGE by JOHS. B. WIST, translated by SIGVALD STOYLEN   *page* 38

III   OUR CULTURAL POSSIBILITIES by WALDEMAR AGER, translated by SIGVALD STOYLEN   *page* 46

IV   PRESERVING OUR MOTHER TONGUE by WALDEMAR AGER, translated by SIGVALD STOYLEN   *page* 55

V   PROPOSALS FOR CONSIDERATION by HERMAN FJELDE, translated by BEN R. EGGAN   *page* 64

VI   THE LANGUAGE IS MOST IMPORTANT by WALDEMAR AGER, translated by LEIF E. HANSEN *page* 68

VII   THE MELTING POT by WALDEMAR AGER, translated by ODD S. LOVOLL *page* 77

VIII   THE MELTING POT AGAIN by A. H. LINDELIE, translated by ODD S. LOVOLL *page* 87

IX   TO MR. A. H. LINDELIE by WALDEMAR AGER, translated by ODD S. LOVOLL *page* 94

X   THE GREAT LEVELING by WALDEMAR AGER, translated by LIV DAHL *page* 101

XI   THE CITIZEN AND THE STATE by WALDEMAR AGER, translated by CARL H. CHRISLOCK *page* 117

XII   WALDEMAR THEODORE AGER, 1869–1941 by KENNETH SMEMO *page* 130

CULTURAL PLURALISM
versus ASSIMILIATION

I

Introduction: The Historical Context

by Carl H. Chrislock

THE centennial anniversary of the Eidsvoll Constitution, May 17, 1914, which had established Norway as an independent nation, was a festive day throughout Norwegian America. Nowhere was the jubilation greater than in the Twin Cities of Minneapolis and St. Paul where the entire weekend was given over to a series of celebrations. A stream of Norwegian Americans began flowing into the metropolitan area on Friday, May 15. Some of the arrivals spent the first day exploring the attractions of urban life; a larger number sought out the headquarters of their various organizations on the grounds of the Minnesota State Fair, the central locale of the three-day observance.

In the afternoon on Saturday, May 16, two simultaneous parades, one originating in downtown Minneapolis and the other in the St. Paul loop, formally opened the festivities. Of the two, the Minneapolis procession seems to have been the more impressive. Long before the scheduled march, the parade route was crowded with spectators, some motivated by ethnic loyalty and others attracted, on an ideal spring day, by the promise of the spectacle. Neither group, it would seem, was disappointed: *Minneapolis Tidende* (Minneapolis Times) called the parade "a magnificent demonstration of Norse organizational activity in Minneapolis." The features most commented on by observers included the colorful regional costumes worn by *bygdelag* paraders; the uniformed musical societies, both vocal and instrumental, who performed competently as they moved along; a Kristianialag contingent attired in the dress of the 1814 Eidsvoll fathers; a group of bearded men in Viking garb aboard a "genuine" Viking ship; and a banner carried by woman suffrage advocates proclaiming, "Women can vote in Norway."

Partly mounted on horses, partly auto-borne, and partly on foot, members of the parade headed toward the lower end of Nicollet Avenue and from there to the east bank of the Mississippi, where the marchers boarded streetcars bound for the fair grounds while the autos proceeded to the same destination. After arriving there, the paraders joined their St. Paul counterparts — who had put on a successful demonstration of their own — for a final march around the grounds. A variety of activities — *bygdelag* festivals, a sentimental reunion of the legendary Norwegian-speaking 15th Wisconsin Civil War Regiment, and a performance of Gunnar Heiberg's *Nei* (No) by members of the University of Minnesota Norse club — filled the time between dispersal of the parade and the convocation of a program in the grandstand at 9:00 P.M. The latter featured dramatic representations of several episodes from Norwegian history, including St. Olaf at Hundorp in Gudbrandsdal, the 1814 Eidsvoll deliberations, and Leif Ericson's landing on the shores of Vinland.

Sunday the 17th marked the high point of the celebration. In the morning local Norwegian-American churches (along with most Norwegian-American churches throughout the United States) adapted their worship services to centennial themes. An afternoon folk festival in the Hippodrome offered several attractions: a 500-voice children's choir attired in red, white and blue; an emotional tribute to a group of Civil War veterans who enjoyed an honored place on the stage behind the banner of the 15th Wisconsin Regiment; a festival address by H. K. Madsen, a well-known Chicago Methodist clergyman; and shorter speeches by prominent Minnesotans. An evening musicale, also in the Hippodrome, wound up the day's program. It featured a combined choir of 1,500 voices directed by F. Melius Christiansen, several of the many Norwegian choral groups of the Twin Cities, and the St. Olaf College band.

Informed critics assigned high marks to the musical performances whose repertoire ranged from patriotic songs and familiar Lutheran hymns to compositions by Grieg, Beethoven, Handel, and Wagner. The speeches deserve less praise, but they, too, were attuned to the spirit of the day. In any case the total impact of the observance was greater than the sum of its parts. Many of the participants were familiar with the festival site, having previously visited the Minnesota State Fair. They may have enjoyed their earlier experiences, but the necessity of coping with an English-speaking milieu may well have inhibited their enjoyment. On this occasion, however, Norwegian speech and Norwegian-American perspectives dominated the proceedings. One could, as *Minneapolis Tidende* pointed out, mingle with a vast Norwegian-speaking crowd and freely exchange 17th of May felicitations or casual conversations about the weather with anyone in sight. The recognition which the jubilee received from non-Norwegians was equally uplifting: the Twin City newspapers, for example, accorded it full coverage in both their news and feature columns. "References to it in later years," writes Odd S. Lovoll, "demonstrated the symbolic value it had for Norwegian Americans. It seemed to reveal their strength and also the fact of their acceptance as part of the American nation."[1]

Although the Twin City observance attracted "the largest gathering of Norwegian Americans ever assembled," it was not the only commemoration of the Eidsvoll anniversary. The Norwegian societies of Madison and Milwaukee organized rallies in their respective cities: Wisconsin Governor Francis McGovern addressed both, appearing in Madison during the afternoon and in Milwaukee the evening of May 17th. A crowd of 5,000 persons attended a program of oratory and song in La Crosse. Chicago Norwegians also celebrated: a feature of their festival arousing particular interest was a children's parade, an imported Norwegian tradition. Such Norwegian-American centers as Fargo, Grand Forks, and Hettinger, in North Dakota, along with Norse communities on the Atlantic seaboard and the Pacific coast, organized festivals which attracted enthusiastic audiences. All in all, one is tempted to wonder how any Norwegian Americans living in proximity to others of their kind could have avoided exposure to their ancestral heritage on May 17, 1914.[2]

---

[1] Odd Sverre Lovoll, *A Folk Epic: The* Bygdelag *in America*, 120 (Boston, 1975); *Minneapolis Tidende*, May 21, 1914. The account is based chiefly on *Tidende's* coverage. All *Tidende* citations are from its weekly edition.

[2] *Minneapolis Tidende*, May 28, 1914.

Fifty or sixty years earlier, few observers would have predicted that as late as 1914 Norwegian Americans would retain the degree of ethnic solidarity manifested in the widespread Eidsvoll centennial festivities. Writing in 1847, when Norwegian settlement in Wisconsin was in its infancy, Ole Munch Ræder, a Norwegian scholar on assignment by his government to study the American jury system, commented on the adaptability of Norwegian immigrants to American conditions. He was particularly impressed by "the great ease with which they learn the English language and, unfortunately, the equal facility they have in forgetting their own as soon as they cease to use it every day. In this respect they seem in no way to differ from their ancestors who, when they had settled in France, forgot their native land . . . and tongue so rapidly that it has been the object of astonishment to historians and literary scholars."[3]

Others shared Ræder's perception. At the outset of his long career as churchman and educator, Laur. Larsen, the pioneer president of Luther College who arrived on American shores in 1857, "looked upon the absorption of the Norwegian immigrants into the American people as a matter of course and as an event of the near future."[4] In defining criteria for awarding a University of Wisconsin scholarship which he endowed in 1876, John A. Johnson, a successful Madison businessman and politician, suggested that until 1900 preference be given to candidates possessing a working knowledge of one of the Scandinavian languages; after that date competition would be open to all students on an equal basis. By then, Johnson believed, "students of Scandinavian descent would be indistinguishable in the stream of American life and should take their place in competition with others."[5]

Notwithstanding the expectation that assimilation would be rapid, Norwegian Americans proceeded early in the settlement period to build a number of cultural institutions. Two were particularly important: the press and the church. Significantly, neither assigned high priority to ethnic preservation. The press assumed a multiple role in Norwegian-American life, but most editors and publishers, some of

[3] Gunnar J. Malmin, tr. and ed., *America in the Forties: The Letters of Ole Munch Ræder*, 33 (Minneapolis, 1929).
[4] Karen Larsen, "The Adjustment of a Pioneer Pastor to American Conditions: Laur. Larsen, 1857–1880," in *Norwegian-American Studies and Records*, 4: 5 (Northfield, Minnesota, 1929).
[5] Agnes M. Larson, *John A. Johnson: An Uncommon American*, 85–86 (Northfield, 1969).

whom nourished ambitions to organize voting blocs, probably regarded their enterprises primarily as agents of acculturation. Although Lutheran churchmen — whose flocks accounted for an overwhelming majority of church-going Norwegian Americans — tended to resist fraternization with Christians of other denominations, they welcomed co-operative arrangements with non-Norwegian Lutherans and indicated a willingness to substitute English for Norwegian as the language of worship whenever such a step would best serve the church's evangelical mission.[6]

The situation in 1900 confounded earlier expectations. Far from having faded away, as would have happened if rapid assimilation had prevailed, the Norwegian-language press was expanding its readership and would continue to do so for another decade and a half. Ethnicity also permeated church life. Norwegian congregations within the national Baptist, Congregational, and Methodist fellowships affiliated with special federations such as the Norwegian-Danish Methodist Conference, an arrangement facilitating retention of Norwegian as the language of worship and religious education. In one sense, the Lutheran church of 1900 was more "ethnic" than it had been half a century earlier. In the 1850s Norwegian Lutheranism had been divided into three major factions: a high-church confessional group organized as the Norwegian Synod; a low-church pietist wing represented by the Eielsen (later Hauge's) Synod; and a "broad church" party affiliated with the Synod of Northern Illinois. Two of the three stood in a co-operative relationship with non-Norwegians. The Synod of Northern Illinois was a multiethnic organization, consisting of Swedish-, Norwegian-, and English-speaking contingents. Although formally a separate entity, the Norwegian Synod had negotiated an arrangement with the German Missouri Synod providing for the education of Norwegian Synod pastors at the latter's seminary, Concordia, an institution located at St. Louis, Missouri.

With the passing of time, these interethnic ties became weaker rather than stronger. In 1860 the Swedish and Norwegian congregations seceded from the Synod of Northern Illinois to form the Scan-

---

[6] Larsen, "The Adjustment of a Pioneer Pastor," 6. On the pioneer Norwegian-American press, see Arlow W. Andersen, *The Immigrant Takes His Stand: The Norwegian-American Press and Public Affairs, 1847–1872* (Northfield, 1953). A standard work on Norwegian Lutheranism is E. Clifford Nelson and Eugene L. Fevold, *The Lutheran Church Among Norwegian-Americans: A History of the Evangelical Lutheran Church*, 2 vols. (Minneapolis, 1960).

dinavian Augustana Synod; ten years later the Swedes and Norwegians negotiated an amicable separation, a move followed by the establishment of two new groupings: the Norwegian Augustana Synod and the Norwegian-Danish Conference. The Norwegian Synod organized its own seminary in 1876. A few years later the outbreak of a bitter doctrinal controversy split the Synod, thereby further compromising the Missouri connection. At the same time, Norwegian remained overwhelmingly the language of worship and communication within all Lutheran churches of Norse origin.

Intensified Norwegian-American organizational activity, already visible in 1900 and considerably more so a decade later, was another sign of the times. A substantial number of Norwegian-American societies — literary, dramatic, temperance, musical, and the like — had appeared on the scene earlier, but with the exception of several temperance and singing societies, few achieved longevity. By contrast the period from 1895 to World War I marked the emergence of several viable organizations, some of which are alive and well in 1977. Nidaros, the first Sons of Norway lodge, was founded in north Minneapolis on January 16, 1895; by 1914 Sons of Norway was a flourishing order consisting of 135 lodges and claiming a membership of 12,000. Primarily a fraternal society which administered an insurance program for the benefit of its members, the order also published *Sønner af Norge* (Sons of Norway), a monthly periodical first appearing in 1904, and sponsored a wide range of cultural events. Daughters of Norway organized its first lodge in 1897; by 1914 it had 3,000 members in forty-one lodges.[7]

A picnic in Minnehaha Park, Minneapolis, on June 25, 1899, arranged for the pleasure and edification of immigrants from the Valdres district of Norway, led two years later to the establishment of Valdres Samband (Union) which in turn marked the birth of the *bygdelag* movement. In Norwegian-American usage, *bygdelag* denotes a society (*lag*) whose members have migrated to North America from a particular district (*bygd*) in Norway. The identifying marks of a *bygd* include neither size nor congruence with a political-administrative subdivision, but rather a distinctive culture possessing its own dialect, songs, folk

[7] Carl [G. O.] Hansen, "Det norske foreningsliv i Amerika," in *Norsk-amerikanernes festskrift 1914*, 282–283 (Decorah, Iowa, 1914). The *Festskrift* was edited by Johs. B. Wist. Hansen, *My Minneapolis*, 156–158 (Minneapolis, 1956), also presents the early history of Sons of Norway.

tales, style of humor, and modes of artistic expression. Although Norway has a small population, the variations among *bygd* cultures are considerable, a reality attributable to geography and terrain.

Since *bygd* loyalty strongly permeated the consciousness of Norwegian Americans, particularly in the first generation, it may not be surprising that the Valdres Samband model found imitators. In late 1909 twelve national *bygdelags* were in existence, and shortly the founding of new ones "reached the proportions of an epidemic." By 1914 the annual *bygdelag* reunion, a two- or three-day event celebrating various aspects of *bygd* tradition and providing the occasion for pleasurable informal socializing, had become a highly visible feature of Norwegian-American life, and one which attracted the involvement of more persons of the first generation than any other secular ethnic activity.[8]

While the *bygdelag* movement was expanding its following, an organization of somewhat different orientation appeared on the scene. On January 28, 1903, a group of one hundred Norwegian Americans, meeting in Minneapolis, resolved to create The Norwegian Society of America (Det Norske Selskab i Amerika). Unlike the *bygdelags*, whose explicit goal was the cultivation of regionalism, the Norwegian Society hoped to "unite all Norwegian Americans around the worthwhile cause of Norwegian language, literature and immigrant history." Spokesmen for the organization sought to allay suspicions of elitism, stressing instead the theme of unity. One friendly press report asserted that the charter membership broadly represented all elements within the Norwegian-American community — "Prohibitionists, Socialists, Democrats, Republicans . . . farmers, artists, clergymen, professors, physicians, musicians, workers, editors, salesmen, merchants and students," as well as persons of varying religious persuasions.[9]

In terms of popularity, the Norwegian Society failed to achieve the spectacular success of the *bygdelags*: in 1914 its roster registered a paid-up membership of only four hundred.[10] Apparently it never managed to erase the image of elitism, and the persistence of *bygd* loyalty within the Norwegian-American community may have inhibited its campaign to nourish a broader Norwegian-American loyalty. Neverthe-

[8] Lovoll, *A Folk Epic*, 24–32, 67, 90.
[9] Lloyd Hustvedt, *Rasmus Bjørn Anderson: Pioneer Scholar*, 240 (Northfield, 1966); *Reform* (Eau Claire, Wisconsin), February 3, 1903.
[10] *Minneapolis Tidende*, January 8, 1914.

less, it left a record of accomplishments. For one thing, it sponsored *Kvartalskrift* (Quarterly), the periodical which initially published the articles translated for the present volume. For another, it encouraged Norwegian language maintenance, partly through an annual Norse declamation contest, and partly by co-operating with other groups on behalf of expanded Norwegian instruction in the public schools. Finally it stimulated the creativity of a number of aspiring writers and artists through an awards program and, more intangibly, by according recognition to cultural activity.

In addition to Sons of Norway, Daughters of Norway, the *bygdelags*, and the Norwegian Society, a number of other significant Norwegian ethnic organizations came into being in the late 19th and in the early 20th century. Nordmanns-Forbundet (The League of Norsemen), a federation which aimed to solidify the cultural ties binding Norwegians in the home country to their overseas kinsmen, was founded in 1907; by 1914 it claimed a membership of more than twenty thousand in North America and about the same in Norway. Ygdrasil, a Wisconsin society founded in Madison in 1896, catered to Norwegian Americans who entertained a serious interest in Norwegian history, literature, and contemporary affairs. The Symra Society of Decorah, Iowa, founded in 1907, was similarly oriented, as were parallel organizations in such Norwegian-American centers as Chicago and Minneapolis.[11]

A noticeable broadening of ethnic activity accompanied the proliferation of organizations that became so visible after the turn of the century. Two examples have been mentioned: the annual *bygdelag* reunions and the 1914 festivities which to a large extent were organized under *bygdelag* auspices. A host of other activities also were pursued. The process of collecting a centennial gift to be presented to Norway on July 4, 1914, was a major preoccupation for several years before the Eidsvoll anniversary. Music festivals, a tradition inherited from the 19th century, attracted the participation of vocal and instrumental groups from all over the nation. The temperance crusade, another carry-over from the 19th century, took on renewed intensity.[12]

---

[11] Letter of Wilhelm Morgenstierne to *Minneapolis Tidende*, April 9, 1914. See also the issue of September 16, 1916; *Normanden* (Grand Forks, North Dakota), January 11, 1916. See also Peer Strømme's account of Ygdrasil, in his column, "Fra det ene til det andet," in *Normanden*, March 18, 1919. The Minneapolis organization was called "Norwegian Society of Minneapolis." *Minneapolis Tidende*, May 13, 1915, carried an account of its annual banquet.

[12] On delivery of *mindegaven* (the centennial gift), see *Minneapolis Tidende*, July

INTRODUCTION

Another campaign that generated considerable steam was the drive to establish Norwegian-language instruction within the American educational system. Like the temperance crusade this, too, had 19th century antecedents: Rasmus B. Anderson had pioneered a Scandinavian-studies program at the University of Wisconsin in the 1870s, and in the following years other institutions of higher learning (exclusive of church-related Norwegian-American colleges) had followed Wisconsin's example. In the early 1900s the campaign was broadened to include elementary and secondary schools. A degree of success rewarded this effort, particularly in Minnesota, North Dakota, and Wisconsin.[13]

Data assembled by the Society for the Advancement of Scandinavian Study for the years from 1912 to 1914 indicate a 65 per cent enrollment increase in courses in Scandinavian language and culture at the twenty American colleges offering Swedish and the thirty-two offering Norwegian. In both instances, church-related colleges such as St. Olaf and Gustavus Adolphus were not included. On the secondary level, five high schools had introduced Scandinavian language instruction for the first time in 1910; four years later, twenty-eight high schools, most of them in Minnesota and North Dakota, were offering Norwegian and Swedish to 1,190 students. Taking advantage of a Minnesota law of 1907 which permitted five hours of foreign-language instruction per week in elementary schools, proponents of Norwegian also made an impact on the grade-school level. According to one computation based on official reports from thirty-two of Minnesota's eighty-seven counties, Norse was taught "in 103 grade and country schools" during the 1913–1914 year.[14]

Objective analysts might doubt that this limited progress constituted a trend, but persons who wanted to believe in *norskdommen's* future were elated.[15] An advertisement issued in 1914 by *Ungdom-*

23, 1914; on its disposition, see *Tidende*, January 21, 1915. Hansen, *My Minneapolis*, 185–223.

[13] Hustvedt, *Rasmus Bjørn Anderson*, 89–122; editorial in *Lutheraneren* (Minneapolis), January 8, 1913.

[14] *Minneapolis Tidende*, May 6, 1914, reported on the annual meeting of the Society for the Advancement of Scandinavian Study. Summary of a report of the Society for the Advancement of Scandinavian Study, in *Minneapolis Tidende*, February 12, 1914; J. N. Lenker, *Tal dit modersmaal: A Popular Appeal in Three Languages for a Three-Language Education, English, Scandinavian, German*, n.p. (Minneapolis, 1914).

[15] The term *norskdom* may be translated freely as Norwegianness, and it indicates things Norwegian in the broadest sense. When the definite article *-en* (the) is added so that it becomes *norskdommen*, the noun, as used here and by immigrant writers, may be interpreted to mean "Norway in America," i.e., the transfer and retention of a distinct Norwegian subculture in the New World.

mens Ven (The Friend of Youth) a semimonthly religious paper published in Minneapolis, proclaimed the arrival of a renaissance: "Until recently it was a common belief that the Norwegian language would inside of a few years be as dead as a door nail. We could already hear the funeral bells peal out their mournful notes as it slowly and solemnly was being carried to its final resting place.

"But now, instead of a funeral, we are witnessing the march of triumph. Not only in the church schools, but in the common schools and the high schools throughout the Northwest, the Norwegian language has been introduced and is being studied, not only by young persons of Norwegian descent, but even by Yankees, Irishmen, and Jews."[16]

Ethnic partisanship coupled with a desire to build circulation undoubtedly influenced the perspective of the editor of *Ungdommens Ven*. On the other hand, the degree to which Norwegian Americans still retained a consciousness of their identity also invalidated earlier assumptions that Norwegian assimilation into the mainstream of American society would be instantaneous. Such assumptions obviously failed to take a number of factors into account. And normal curiosity prompts an inevitable question: what were these factors?[17]

First of all, until World War I, a continuing stream of immigrants reinforced Norwegianness within an American community. Charts depicting the course of immigration show that migration from Norway to the United States crested in 1882, but also that thousands of new arrivals landed in the early 1890s and the first decade of the 20th century. In fact, records of the United States Immigration Commission register the arrival of nearly as many Norwegians in the period from 1902 through 1905 as from 1881 through 1884, the tally being 73,332 and 75,249, respectively.[18]

Second, Norwegian settlement in the United States tended to concentrate in compact, homogeneous communities, a pattern obviously favorable to ethnic preservation. The difference between communities

[16] Lenker, *Tal dit modersmaal*.
[17] The literature on this problem is extensive. Two good studies are: Peter A. Munch, "Segregation and Assimilation of Norwegian Settlements in Wisconsin," in *Norwegian-American Studies and Records*, 18: 102–140; and Torben Krontoft, "Factors in Assimilation: A Comparative Study," in *Norwegian-American Studies*, 26: 184–205.
[18] Carlton C. Qualey, *Norwegian Settlement in the United States*, 251 (Northfield, 1938).

that maintained "ethnic purity" and those engulfed by non-Norwegian neighbors suggests the importance of this factor. By 1918, for example, seventy-five years after the Norwegian settlements in southeastern Wisconsin were established, Muskego, located in the midst of an ethnically heterogeneous area near Milwaukee, had substantially abandoned Norwegian as the language of daily speech, and English predominated as the language of worship in local Norwegian Lutheran churches. On the other hand, the Koshkonong community in Dane County, which was more isolated than Muskego from non-Scandinavian influences, remained staunchly Norwegian both in speech and worship.[19]

More subtle factors were also operative. A Norwegian caught in the grip of "America fever" might have imagined that adopting a new mode of existence would be simple, and a refreshing contrast to the misery of Norway in the 19th century. However, upon arriving in North America, the immigrant possibly experienced a longing for some vestige of the old life style. Histories of Norwegian congregations no doubt exaggerate the piety of the pioneer fathers and mothers, but unquestionably many immigrants discovered previously unsuspected religious and cultural needs after coming to the United States, needs which usually could not be satisfied within the context of American church life.

On this point the testimony of Herman Amberg Preus, a founding father of the Norwegian Synod and an acute, if not disinterested, observer of Norwegian-American life, is revealing. In a work published nearly twenty-five years after his arrival in the United States, Preus characterized the religious consciousness of ordinary Norwegian immigrants as a paradoxical combination. On the one hand, it revealed spiritual indifference and ignorance. On the other, he described this religious consciousness as having an outward respect for the sacred and also a tenacious adherence to the ancestral faith. Separation from the security of Norway apparently accentuated the latter attitudes. At any rate, immigrants who settled in the American West soon experienced a profound desire for familiar arrangements in the realm of "church, minister and school." American churches might exist in the neighborhood, but language and doctrinal differences rendered these religious

[19] Einar Haugen, "The Struggle over Norwegian," in *Norwegian-American Studies and Records*, 17:4–6.

institutions in the New World unsatisfactory to Norwegian settlers. The only remaining recourse was to support the organization of a Norwegian Lutheran church.[20]

The analysis made by Preus can also be applied to such secular institutions as the press and the *bygdelags*; like the church, their reason for being was to satisfy an immigrant need for the familiar. And once these institutions were established, they became a force working for the maintenance of ethnic identity. This was obviously true of the church even though Lutheran spokesmen consistently proclaimed the priority of the church's evangelical mission over any ethnic entanglement. It was equally true of the press. Writing in 1914, Gisle Bothne, professor of Scandinavian languages and literature at the University of Minnesota, attributed the sturdy vitality of *norskdommen* in North America largely to the influence of such newspapers as *Decorah-Posten* in Iowa and *Skandinaven* in Chicago.[21]

The vicissitudes of an overseas homeland have often encouraged ethnic group consciousness within the United States. To a lesser extent than their Czech, Polish, or Irish counterparts, but nevertheless unmistakably, Norwegian Americans also have been influenced by this factor. In the 1880s several immigrant societies launched fund drives on behalf of the Liberal party in Norway and of its crusade to establish parliamentary supremacy within the Norwegian constitutional system. Twenty years later there began to mount a Norwegian dissatisfaction with the 1814 joint monarchy arrangement, which placed Norway and Sweden under the sovereignty of the House of Bernadotte. The union had its basis in approximate juridical equality, but Norway was definitely the junior partner in the twin monarchy. Tension escalated to the point of crisis in the spring of 1905, when on a constitutional pretext the Norwegian Parliament repudiated the nation's allegiance to King Oscar II. Reluctant Swedish acceptance of the Norwegian action peaceably resolved the crisis; Norway now became a fully independent country with its own monarchy.

Norwegian Americans reacted exuberantly to the events of 1905. By coincidence, the Norwegian Society of America was assembled in

---

[20] John N. Kildahl, "*Et sidste ord i debatten om navneforandringen,*" in *Lutheraneren*, May 7, 1919; Olaf M. Norlie, ed., *Norsk lutherske prester i Amerika*, 19 (Minneapolis, 1915), quotes H. A. Preus, *Syv foredrag om de kirkelige forholde blandt de norske i Amerika* (1875).

[21] In a review of *Norsk-amerikanernes festskrift 1914*, *Minneapolis Tidende*, March 19, 1914.

Fargo, North Dakota, for its third annual meeting in early June when the crisis was passing through its decisive phase. The impact of arriving press dispatches on the gathering was, to say the least, enlivening. Festivities sponsored by the Society on June 6 and 7 drew crowds that numbered "between six and eight thousand . . . and virtually every building in Fargo displayed a Norwegian flag, and some were completely adorned with flags."

An article by Johs. B. Wist published in *Kvartalskrift* six months later interpreted the longer-range impact of 1905 on Norwegians in America. According to Wist, "the 'bloodless revolution' in Norway had drawn the attention of the whole world, and not least that of the great American nation, to the land of our origin." Previously Norway had received only slight coverage in the American press; during the year of the coming of independence, happenings in Norway had commanded large headlines and comprehensive treatment in the news columns of leading American newspapers. In short, "America had discovered Norway" — and obviously admired the object of its discovery. Norwegian Americans were now basking in the approval of their fellow citizens.

More important from Wist's standpoint, they also had gained an enhanced respect for their ancestral heritage. He reported that during the summer of 1905 persons formerly indifferent to their Norse origin suddenly "found themselves busy seeking a place on the band wagon." Promising vistas now lay open. The events of 1905, he concluded, "strengthened our faith in ourselves, built confidence in our own capacities as a nationality, and enriched our intellectual life. Translated into individual terms, this means that he and she have acquired a heightened sense of human worth. It follows that we are more effectively equipped than before to meet our responsibilities within American society."[22]

Still another factor facilitated Norwegian-American activity — and indeed all ethnic activity — early in the century: a permissive national climate. As Professor John Higham points out, the attitude of mainstream America toward the "outsider" has oscillated between intolerant rejection (in common parlance, "nativism" or "knownothingism") and benevolent acceptance. The early and middle 1890s, years of economic depression and "psychic crisis," witnessed strident de-

[22] *Kvartalskrift*, 1:21 (July, 1905), 2: 4–5 (January, 1906).

mands in America for restriction on immigration, a militant anti-Catholic crusade, and a tendency to link aliens with radicalism. In the late 1890s the benevolent stance staged a comeback that persisted through the early years of the Progressive era. During this period, which Higham calls an "Age of Confidence," the drive for immigration restriction abated and social reformers encouraged the children of immigrants to respect the life styles of their parents. By 1910 the tolerance marking the Age of Confidence had begun to erode. The campaign to exclude illiterate immigrants revived, "Anglo-Saxon racism" gained new converts, and overt anti-Catholic movements resurfaced.[23]

It is not apparent that this resurgence of nativism materially hampered Norwegian-American ethnic activity. Scandinavians were overwhelmingly Protestant, most potential Scandinavian immigrants were literate, and Anglo-Saxon racism assigned Norwegians, Swedes, Danes, and Icelanders (if not Finns) an exalted place in the hierarchy of races.[24] However, it may not be accidental that such societies as Sons and Daughters of Norway, the *bygdelags*, and Nordmanns-Forbundet originated and got off to a flourishing start within the time span of the Age of Confidence. It also is clear that the climate which developed after the outbreak of war in Europe on August 1, 1914, seriously manacled all ethnic activity, a point discussed at length later.

Prolonged exposure to Norwegian-American sources could tempt an unwary researcher to conclude that by 1914 the Norse-American way of life was becoming more than a series of temporary improvisations bridging the gap between Norway and North America. Such a researcher in fact may have acquired the impression that a respectable Norwegian subculture might have emerged had not the aberrant nativism of the World War I years distorted the normal course of American development. The temptation should be resisted because the thesis is questionable. The Great War obviously had a shattering

[23] John Higham, *Strangers in the Land: Patterns of American Nativism 1860–1925*, 68–193 (New York, 2nd edition, 1973).

[24] At least some Norwegian-American papers tended to support the literacy law. See editorials in *Normanden*, January 27, 1915, and in *Lutheraneren*, February 21, 1917. The case usually made was that Scandinavian immigration would be affected only minimally, since Scandinavian literacy was high. Opinion on the propriety of supporting *The Menace*, a virulently anti-Catholic publication of the prewar period, was divided. Ole L. Kirkeberg, a pro-*norskdom* clergyman, bitterly opposed the periodical in *Lutheraneren*, March 18, 1914. At least one other clergyman, E. Jensen, took sharp issue with Kirkeberg, in *Lutheraneren*, April 8, 1914.

impact on all ethnic activity within the United States, but, even before its outbreak, a number of vulnerabilities menaced the long-range prospects of *norskdommen*.

For one thing, a vast majority of Norwegian Americans were nonparticipants in any form of ethnic activity. Writing in 1914, Carl G. O. Hansen guessed that the membership of all secular societies was approximately 60,000 compared to 15,000 in 1899. A four-fold increase over a fifteen-year period is impressive, but 60,000 constituted a relatively small minority in a population that by 1910 was estimated at 1,500,000, a figure embracing all living Norwegian immigrants and their descendants. According to Odd S. Lovoll, the *bygdelag* movement "seems . . . to have directly touched annually at least 15 per cent of the Norwegian-born." Like Hansen's tally, this calculation equals 60,000, but since it involves only a single activity, it implies a higher level of participation — but obviously it also indicates that 85 per cent of the first generation was not directly touched by *bygdelag* influence.[25]

The availability of a wide range of amenities and opportunities within the larger society partly explains the indifference of most Norwegian Americans to ethnic activity. Executive suites were not overstaffed with Scandinavian Americans, and a few second-generation Norwegians grumbled about a Yankee monopoly in higher education, but access to most professions was open. It is noteworthy, too, that Norwegian Americans who had achieved success in such fields as business, the professions, and politics were not conspicuous advocates of an independent Norwegian-American culture. The politicians made little effort to conceal their national identities when bidding for Scandinavian electoral support, but few of them questioned the melting-pot ethos. Antiassimilationists like Waldemar Ager saw in Senator Knute Nelson of Minnesota the living embodiment of a sturdy Norse ethnicity which the melting pot would irretrievably destroy, thereby depriving American political culture of a valuable asset. Nelson may have appreciated the accolade, but throughout a long career he remained a staunch assimilationist.[26]

High geographic mobility also worked against the maintenance of ethnic consciousness. As of 1914, several of the compact rural

[25] "Det norske foreningsliv i Amerika," in *Festskrift*, 290–291; Lovoll, *A Folk Epic*, 67.

[26] Martin W. Odland, *The Life of Knute Nelson*, 244–245 (Minneapolis, 1926).

neighborhoods in southern Wisconsin remained steadfastly Norwegian, but their surplus population had long since begun a movement into other areas. Part of the out-migration, augmented by fresh arrivals from Norway, established new homogeneous communities further west, but a portion of it settled in the ethnically mixed milieu of cities large and small. Meanwhile Norwegian urban concentrations in such metropolitan centers as Chicago and Minneapolis were beginning to disperse, a process well underway by 1914.

Another sign of the times that alarmed the friends of *norskdommen* was a growing inclination by Lutheran leaders to reexamine the linkages between Norwegian ethnicity and the church. In 1914 Norwegian still predominated as the language of worship in all the Norwegian Lutheran synods, but a pronounced trend toward English was discernible, particularly in urban congregations. Several prominent churchmen supported the trend. In his official message to the 1913 convention of the United Lutheran Church, the largest Norwegian church body, President Theodor H. Dahl forcefully advocated encouragement of "the English work." Failure to do so, Dahl argued, could only facilitate a mass defection from Lutheranism by the third and fourth generations.[27]

The implications of Dahl's recommendation were far-reaching. So long as the Lutheran congregations remained "ethnic," more than 500,000 Norwegian Americans retained at least one institutional tie with their ancestral heritage. Moreover, the Lutheran churches provided the Norwegian community with a number of essential support services not readily available elsewhere. These included elementary instruction in Norwegian for the young under the tutelage of the congregational schoolmaster, competently taught courses in the Norwegian language and culture in church-supported academies and colleges, coverage of ethnic happenings in church papers, and use of the facilities of such church-related enterprises as Augsburg Publishing House and the Folkebladet Publishing Company, both of which published or distributed secular as well as devotional literature.

Another uncertainty confronting *norskdommen* was the orientation of Norwegian-American youth. Encouragement could be derived from the addition of Scandinavian language and culture courses to the public school curriculum, but opportunities to enroll in these courses were

[27] *Beretning om det fireogtyvende aarsmøde for Den forenede norsk lutherske kirke i Amerika avholdt i St. Paul Minnesota fra 12te til 18te juni 1913*, 62 (Minneapolis, 1913).

open to only a small minority of Norwegian-American school children. One might suspect, too, that proponents of Scandinavian studies exaggerated the potential of their favorite programs. After touring the United States for the purpose of investigating the linguistic situation in immigrant communities, one Norwegian journalist flatly disputed the claims being advanced. In his view, only the children of families affluent enough to finance a Scandinavian tour had developed any enthusiasm for Scandinavian studies; most of the others were either indifferent or downright hostile. He also reported that the securing of funds for maintaining Scandinavian instruction in the public schools of Chicago was a yearly crusade by the Norwegian and Swedish newspapers of that city.[28]

Responses to a questionnaire, sent by the Society for the Advancement of Scandinavian Study to forty presiding officials of high schools offering Scandinavian programs in 1913, left a somewhat less pessimistic (but by no means completely reassuring) impression. Eleven respondents indicated that Scandinavians residing in their districts supported the programs; ten replied in an opposite vein. Fourteen reported that the programs were popular among the students enrolled; only two complained of indifference. Finally, most of the enrolled students had chosen the courses, not of their own free will, but in deference to parental wishes.[29]

In addition to other vulnerabilities, a basic lack of unity and sense of direction within the ethnic organizational sector further compromised the prospects of Norwegian-American culture. One faction preferred to function within a Lutheran context; an opposing group was more ecumenical. Some activists believed ethnic consciousness could exist independently of the Norwegian language; others contended that discarding the Norse tongue would sacrifice all. The *bygdelag* focus was based on a regional folk culture; a number of other societies sought to encourage "high" culture marked by a national rather than a regional orientation. Most important of all was the division between "pluralists" and "assimilationists." Firmly believing in the possibility of a viable Norwegian-American culture, the former wanted to work for the emergence of such a culture. The assimilationists, on the other hand,

[28] The article originally appeared in *Fædrelandsvennen* of Kristiansand and was reprinted in *Normanden*, October 5, 1915.
[29] Summary of a publication by the Society for the Advancement of Scandinavian Study, *Minneapolis Tidende*, February 12, 1914.

favored a course of action designed to facilitate complete (if not immediate) integration of Norwegian Americans into the mainstream of American society.

The house-divided theme also permeates the history of the Norwegian Society of America. Its constituting session, held in Minneapolis on January 28, 1903, was enlivened by a spirited disagreement on the Lutheran issue. After convening the meeting, Rasmus B. Anderson, a pioneer promoter of Norwegian-American culture who more recently had assumed the role of a cranky nay-sayer, moved that voting rights be limited to Lutherans in good standing. In so doing, he defied a preliminary understanding which specified that membership should be open to all men and women committed to the maintenance of Norwegian cultural traditions in North America. The assembly overwhelmingly rejected this motion, whereupon Anderson seceded both from the meeting and the projected society.

Apparently the effect of Anderson's action was minimal. Following his departure, the meeting voted the Norwegian Society of America into existence, adopted a draft of a constitution (formulated in advance), and elected a slate of officers which included, among others, two Lutheran ministers and a prominent Unitarian clergyman, Amandus E. Norman. Within the Norwegian-American community at large, Anderson's impact was equally faint. While the conservative Norwegian Synod "remained aloof" from the Society, an agreeable relationship was established with clergy of the United Church.[30]

The relationship between the Norwegian Society and the emerging *bygdelag* movement was less amiable. Perhaps this is understandable. Committed as it was to the promotion of national culture, the Society "found the divisive implications of [*bygdelag*] regionalism distasteful." Other circumstances reinforced this natural antipathy. In 1906 officials of the Society formulated a complex strategy designed to place *bygdelag* leadership in their hands. The scheme soon collapsed, giving way to a cool, reserved coexistence between the two organizations. *Bygdelag* members could not affiliate with the Society and remain in good standing in their own group, and vice versa. However, an occasional exchange of recriminations continued.[31]

[30] Hustvedt, *Rasmus Bjørn Anderson*, 262–271; *Reform*, February 3, 1903.
[31] Lovoll, *A Folk Epic*, 51. See a letter of L. O. Thorpe, a prominent Norwegian Society member, to *Minneapolis Tidende*, April 15, 1915.

Meanwhile, the Norwegian Society had become active in causes more creative than the feud with the *bygdelag*. *Kvartalskrift*, its official quarterly, was established in 1905. The appearance of this periodical not only heightened the Society's visibility but also provided a forum in which controversies could be aired and significant aspects of the Norwegian-American experience interpreted. As might be expected, the magazine clearly reflected the personality and commitments of Waldemar Ager, its editor. On the other hand, the columns of *Kvartalskrift* were open to a variety of opinions, a reality underscored by the selections in the present volume.

The first issue carried an article by Johs. B. Wist seeking to clarify the Norwegian Society's role. (See Wist's essay, page 38.) The tendency of Wist's reasoning is decidedly assimilationist. Surrounded as they were by powerful alien influences, Norwegian Americans could never hope to create an independent culture or literature of their own. In due time they would fully merge with other elements in the nation's varied population, and in the process participate in the shaping of a genuine American culture which, according to the author, had not yet developed. In the meantime, groups like the Norwegian Society were vested with a significant responsibility: to maintain a link with Norwegian culture, thereby minimizing the intellectual and aesthetic deprivation of a people in transition from one identity to another.

A response by Ager, published in the next issue of *Kvartalskrift*, disagrees fundamentally with Wist's argument. (See Ager's essay, page 46.) In the editor's view, assimilation eventually engulfed Norwegian Americans; self-respect demanded that they leave "independent cultural traces" bearing witness to their existence and experience. Turning to another Wist premise, Ager affirms the inability of modern Norwegian literature to serve Norwegian Americans, who "in a literary sense" were still dominated by an early nineteenth century outlook. Moreover, Ager contends, conditions were ripe for the emergence of an independent literature. Norwegian-American history contained a storehouse of experience from which the creative artist could draw. The material foundations of life had been laid, and such basic institutions as church and school were functioning in their spheres. The editor concedes that there was a language problem, but he points to the ability of ethnic Swedes residing in Finland to produce a literature in Swedish and to the persistence of Norwegian speech in the United but a trend toward qualitative improvement was discernible. According to Ager, the development of any literary tradition usually was marked by a progression from simple versification and polemical tracts to achievement of a more mature level of performance. Such a progression, he contends, was clearly visible in the case of Norwegian-American writing.

Unfortunately, the reading audience remained unresponsive. Whatever time and affection Norwegian Americans could spare from material pursuits was being lavished on the church and politics. The effect on writers was devastating. They were doomed to poverty and deprived of the creative stimulation generated by intimate rapport with an audience. However, a few signs of hope dotted the horizon. Enthusiasm for immigrant history was growing, the *bygdelags* were flourishing, and a new interest in the Norwegian language and culture was surfacing. The encouragement which one could derive from these signs, Ager seems to imply, justified a modest degree of optimism with respect to the future of Norwegian-American literature and culture.[33]

A year later Ager's optimism, cautious though it was, appeared less realistic. If the general acceptability of ethnic diversity within the United States was diminishing by 1914, the climate fostered by World War I significantly strengthened that trend. Few Americans expected or desired to have the United States participate in the military conflict, but the situation nevertheless bred a sense of national peril. Contrary to an assumption which the exuberant confidence of the Progressive era had encouraged, it was now clear that "civilized" nations could still perpetrate mass slaughter on each other — a perception which called attention to an imperative need for national solidarity. Two threats appeared to menace such solidarity: a highly organized German-American effort to divert American foreign policy from an allegedly pro-Ally course; and the slow pace of "Americanization" within the ethnic communities peopled by recent immigrants from southern and eastern Europe.[34]

Nervous patriots undoubtedly exaggerated the situation, but a sense of danger throughout the nation sustained the rise of a campaign designed to transform Polish, Swedish, Italian, and particularly German Americans, along with all other United States citizens of the

[33] Waldemar Ager, "Norsk-amerikansk skjønliteratur," in *Festskrift*, 292–306.
[34] Higham, *Strangers in the Land*, 194–204.

"hyphenated" category, into "unhyphenated Americans" of the 100 percent variety — a campaign popularly called the "anti-hyphenist" crusade. Speaking to a group of recently naturalized citizens gathered in Philadelphia's Convention Hall on May 10, 1915, President Woodrow Wilson pointedly reminded his listeners of the obligations now resting on them: "And while you bring all the countries with you, you come with a purpose of leaving all other countries behind you — bringing what is best of their spirit, but not looking over your shoulders and seeking to perpetuate what you intended to leave behind in them. . . . You cannot dedicate yourself to America unless you become in every respect and with every purpose of your will thorough Americans. You cannot become thorough Americans if you think of yourselves in groups. America does not consist of groups. A man who thinks of himself as belonging to a particular national group in America has not yet become an American. . . ."[35]

Utilizing both the written and spoken word, Theodore Roosevelt was preaching the same message in more strident language than Wilson. An address to a Knights of Columbus gathering in Carnegie Hall, New York, on October 12, 1915, capsuled the ex-President's line. "During the last year and a quarter," Roosevelt told the Knights, "it has been brought home to us in startling fashion that many of the elements of our nation are not yet properly fused." He went on to emphasize that the "malign activity" of German and Austrian Embassy officials was not the only source of concern. Recently the Imperial Russian government had announced an intention of establishing a center in New York "to foster the Russian language and keep alive the national feeling in immigrants who came hither." Such activity was intolerable. As Roosevelt saw it: "The one absolutely certain way of bringing this nation to ruin . . . would be to permit it to become a tangle of squabbling nationalities, an intricate knot of German Americans, Irish Americans, English Americans, French Americans, Scandinavian Americans or Italian Americans, each preserving its separate nationality, each at heart feeling more sympathy with Europeans of that nationality than with other citizens of the American Republic. The men who do not become Americans and nothing else are hyphenated Americans; and there ought to be no room for them in this country."

Stern as Roosevelt's rhetoric may appear, he did not propose a mass

[35] *A Compilation of the Messages and Papers of the Presidents*, 17: 8066–8067 (New York, n.d.).

deportation of aliens. He did not even recommend exclusion of illiterate immigrants (those unable to read or write any language) who signified a willingness to learn English. However, he did insist that American national security rested not only on military preparedness but also on three other basic foundations: "a common language, English . . . ; a common civil standard, similar ideals, beliefs and customs symbolized by the oath of allegiance to America; and . . . a high standard of living" along with "reasonable equality of opportunity and . . . social and industrial justice." This statement of priorities basically reflected antihyphenist thinking. Some persons favoring this philosophy did not perceive "social and industrial justice" as an essential component of the "Americanization" effort, but virtually all agreed with Roosevelt on the significance of the English language and a common body of "ideals, beliefs and customs."[36]

The rise of antihyphenism threatened Scandinavian Americans less than it did several other ethnic groups. Unlike Germany, the Nordic nations were not potential enemies of the United States, and Americanizers generally regarded Scandinavian immigrants as being more "assimilable" than the peoples of southern and eastern Europe. On the other hand, Scandinavian Americans were not completely out of the line of fire. Measured by antihyphenist norms, the language transition was proceeding too slowly, and President Wilson's strictures against the maintenance of immigrant group consciousness, if interpreted literally, called into question the legitimacy of such organizations as the *bygdelags*, Sons of Norway, and Nordmanns-Forbundet.

Norwegian Americans responded to the campaign for Americanization with various voices. Believing — or pretending to believe — that antihyphenism did not threaten them, some to a greater or lesser degree, identified with the movement. Senator Knute Nelson of Minnesota, whose prestige topped that of any other Norwegian American, discounted both the possibility and desirability of an instantaneous language transition; at the same time, however, he endorsed the notion that liberty was better served in English-speaking lands than elsewhere. The senator also supported strong military preparedness, an uncompromising defense of American rights, and a policy of firmness toward Germany — positions generally linked with antihyphenism. In March, 1916, he voted against the Gore-McLemore

[36] Theodore Roosevelt, *Fear God and Take Your Own Part*, 362, 368, 370 (New York, 1916).

joint congressional resolution warning Americans against taking passage on ships of belligerent nations bound for war zones — a resolution defeated in both houses of Congress by narrow margins. The contrast between Nelson's stand and that of his Minnesota colleagues, all of whom voted for the Gore-McLemore resolution, evoked comment within Anglo-American circles. On March 22, 1916, the influential *New York Times* affirmed: "The Minnesota delegation in Congress consists of eleven Kaiserists and one American, and a mighty fine one, Senator Knute Nelson, born in Norway. . . . Knute Nelson is the only man, the sole American, Minnesota has in Congress." At about the same time that this editorial appeared, a Republican rally in Massachusetts entertained Nelson as guest of honor; the master of ceremonies introduced him as "a citizen who has no hyphen in his system." [37]

Not all politicians of Norse background followed the same course as Nelson. In fact the other Norwegian Americans serving in the 64th Congress — eight in all — voted for the Gore-McLemore bill, thus placing themselves under the *New York Times* ban. However, the image of Nelson as Norwegian America's special representative was strong enough to provide the community with a bit of protective coloration. [38]

Meanwhile a spirited discussion of hyphenism and related issues filled the editorial and letter columns of Norwegian-American newspapers. Nearly all participants explicitly or implicitly accepted the validity of one fundamental proposition: that the oath of allegiance taken at the time of naturalization effected a complete and unconditional transfer of civic loyalty from the homeland to the United States. This oath, however, did not surrender the right to utilize a mother tongue in daily speech or to remain in touch with a homeland culture. The question seemed to be: To what degree did the Wilson-Roosevelt crusade against the hyphen imperil Norwegian-American exercise of this reserved right? One group was inclined to perceive the danger as clear and present. Another tended to minimize the threat without

[37] Odland, *Life of Knute Nelson*, 258, 288.
[38] For the House vote, see *Congressional Record*, 64th Congress, 2nd session, 3720. The eight politicians generally claimed by the Norwegian-American community are: Sydney Anderson, Carl C. Van Dyke, Halvor Steenerson and Andrew J. Volstead of Minnesota; Asle J. Grønna and Henry T. Helgesen of North Dakota; Gilbert N. Haugen of Iowa; and John M. Nelson of Wisconsin. Anderson was of mixed Swedish-Norwegian ancestry and Congressman Van Dyke is counted by virtue of his mother's Norwegian origin.

dismissing it and to accept the need for an Americanization effort, given Imperial Germany's inclination to expect the allegiance of emigrated nationals.[39]

Three Norwegian-language papers in the Upper Midwest emerged as conspicuous champions of the "clear and present danger" thesis. They were *Fram* (Forward) of Fargo, edited by Peter Myrvold; *Sønner af Norge*, then under the editorial direction of Lauritz Stavnheim; and Waldemar Ager's *Reform*. Myrvold and Stavnheim characterized the antihyphenist campaign as a revival of "hysterical Knownothingism," a passing phenomenon perhaps, but one which presently threatened Scandinavian Americans along with all non-Anglo groups.[40] *Reform* interpreted the campaign as a design concocted by Anglo-American politicians for the purpose of culturally "denationalizing" persons of non-English background, thereby reducing them to the level of dependent and manipulable work animals. So long as an ethnic group retained its language and culture, Ager contended, it possessed a weapon capable of resisting such oppression. The editor of *Reform* also denied the reality of an Imperial German threat to American national security; it followed that the German-American campaign to preserve American neutrality was entirely legitimate.

Several Norwegian-American journals took sharp issue with Myrvold, Stavnheim, and Ager. Ignoring a number of implications which might be drawn from Wilson's and Roosevelt's rhetoric, *Normanden* (The Norseman) of Grand Forks, North Dakota, affirmed the nonexistence of any threat to *norskdommen*. Scandinavian Americans were not "hyphenated" citizens; in terms of civic loyalty they were fully American. Unlike Germany, the Scandinavian nations laid no claims on the political loyalty of expatriated nationals; and unlike German Americans, Americans of Scandinavian background acknowledged no such loyalty. The target of antihyphenism was dual citizenship. Nonpolitical cultural activity did not fall within the scope of its concern.

Minneapolis Tidende, one of Norwegian America's three largest papers in terms of circulation, adopted a similar position. Like *Normanden*, it professed distrust of German propaganda and espionage, both of which pointed up the need for an effort toward Americaniza-

---

[39] Charles E. Stangeland, "Bindestreks-amerikanere," in *Nordmands-Forbundet*, 9:397–400 (1916).

[40] Editorials in *Fram*, March 4, May 13, 1915; *Normanden* reprinted a long editorial from *Sønner af Norge* under Stavnheim's by-line on November 9, 1915.

tion. *Tidende* also took pains to guard the reputation and image of Norwegian Americans. In taking note of May 17, 1916, it subordinated customary 17th of May themes to an emphasis on the obligations of Norwegian Americans to their adopted land.

On the other hand, *Tidende* declined to endorse all aspects of the antihyphenist campaign — and here, too, its stance resembled *Normanden's*. It reacted testily to complaints by the *Minneapolis Journal*, occasionally expressed in 1915 and 1916, with respect to the innumerable "foreign-language" churches, fraternal societies, schools, and newspapers in the Upper Midwest which, according to the *Journal*, were impeding the development of patriotism throughout the region. Such complaints, *Tidende* affirmed, missed the point. With a few exceptions, non-English newspapers were in business not to perpetuate Europe in America but to communicate the message of America in a language which their readers could understand. The liquidation of such enterprises would virtually isolate thousands of foreign-born citizens of the United States from all Americanizing influences.[41]

While Norwegian-American editors debated the pros and cons of hyphenism, *Kvartalskrift* was devoting considerable space to one issue raised by the controversy: the efficacy of the American melting pot. By 1916 *The Melting Pot*, Israel Zangwill's flamboyant drama — depicting the amalgamation (under white heat) of oppression-ridden, hate-filled Europeans into a new human species — had become an antihyphenist text. Three essays by Ager and A. H. Lindelie on pages 77–100, all dating from 1916, reflect a profound difference of viewpoint, even within the Norwegian Society of America, concerning Zangwill's theme. Ager and Lindelie have opposing answers to a number of important questions: Was the fusing of all ethnic cultures into a "super" American culture possible and desirable? Or would a variety of cultures serve the nation better? Were those advocating such a fusion willing to accept its implications in their own personal lives? The Ager-Lindelie exchange fails to resolve these questions, but it illuminates the controversy. Perhaps it even sheds some light on a number of stubbornly persistent problems in the history of human relations.

To some degree, the outbreak of war between the United States and Germany on April 6, 1917, temporarily moderated the excesses of

---

[41] *Reform* editorialized frequently on the hyphenism issue. See editorials of July 6, September 7, 28, November 9, December 7, 14, 1915; and May 16, 1916.

antihyphenism. For one thing, the anti-Catholic crusade collapsed, a casualty of the quest for wartime unity. For another, the national administration overtly encouraged ethnic groups with a pro-American orientation to display their identities, a tactic calculated both to build the widest possible support of the war effort and to lend credibility to Wilson's idealistic war aims. Unfortunately, this moderating impact failed to touch all sections and groups. Conservative politicians in the Upper Midwest — where a fresh outbreak of prairie radicalism, under the auspices of the North Dakota Nonpartisan League, had erupted in 1915 — found it more advantageous to link aliens generally with pro-Germanism, disloyalty, and subversion rather than to participate in Wilson's search for national unity, and throughout the country, German Americans obviously found themselves in a more exposed position than before the declaration of war.[42]

The situation facing Norwegian Americans was considerably less ominous. It was even less perilous than that confronting Swedish Americans, whose homeland was popularly regarded as more pro-German in orientation than either Norway or Denmark. A few prominent Norwegian Americans — mostly nonofficeholders — were suspected of harboring pro-German sympathies, but Senator Nelson's solid standing with Anglo-American patriots served as a protective shield. So did the cautious editorial policies of such leading newspapers as *Minneapolis Tidende* and *Skandinaven* of Chicago.

Anxiety nevertheless pervaded the Norwegian-American community. The religious affiliation of most Norwegians created at least a minor embarrassment. "Everyone knows that the Lutheran church originated in Germany, and this does not enhance its popularity here in America at the present time," commented one church paper shortly after America's entrance into the war.[43] Apparent similarities in language and culture further reinforced a tendency to link Scandinavians with Germans. The two groups shared a stock of given names (Hans, Karl, Olga, Helga, for example) and Gothic type predominated in their newspapers and published literature.

The possibility that an uncontrolled and uncontrollable mass hysteria against everything "foreign" might erupt was another hazard. Chauvinistic fanaticism did in fact win a round in Iowa on May 23,

[42] Higham, *Strangers in the Land*, 215–222; Carl H. Chrislock, *The Progressive Era in Minnesota, 1899–1918*, 130–181 (St. Paul, 1971).
[43] Editorial in *Lutheraneren*, May 16, 1917.

1918, when Governor W. L. Harding outlawed oral communication in any language but English; the same thing happened in Nebraska when that state's Council of Defense followed Harding's example. Authorities in Minnesota, Wisconsin, and North Dakota demonstrated more restraint, but in all states and sections patriotic groups generated powerful social sanctions calculated to discourage "foreign speech" on the streets, in the stores, over the telephone, and even in the home. Obviously such a climate did not facilitate Ager's aspiration to rehabilitate Norwegian "among the younger set."

Journalism also faced a perilous situation. To a greater or lesser degree, federal censorship limited the freedom of the press generally, but special regulations governed the circulation of non-English newspapers. Acting on authority conferred by a congressional act of October 6, 1917, President Wilson issued an order requiring editors of non-English journals and periodicals to file an English translation of all political stories and editorials with their local postmaster, who was obliged to block the circulation of any paper failing to comply with the translation requirement. The order provided one escape route: the editor could apply for a presidential permit which, if granted, would place the paper on the same basis as English-language journals. The responsibility of passing on the applications was vested in the postmaster general, a member of the president's cabinet.[44]

As might be expected, the office of Postmaster General Albert S. Burleson soon was deluged with more applications than its limited staff could process. To facilitate action, Burleson solicited the advice of "trustworthy" persons from within the ethnic communities served by the papers submitting applications. He consulted Senator Nelson with respect to the Scandinavian press, a move that undoubtedly speeded the granting of permits but which may not have enhanced freedom of expression. In any case, the war inflicted only minimal casualties on the Norwegian-American press, a fact attributable primarily to scrupulous observance of official edicts and regulations by the journalists themselves.[45]

[44] *Reform*, October 16, 1917, reprinted a long article from *Skandinaven* interpreting the significance of regulations for the Norwegian-American press. The same issue contained an explanation of the regulations of the Minnesota Commission of Public Safety.

[45] Knute Nelson to A. S. Burleson, January 7, 1918, enclosing copy of a letter from Gustav Amlund to Nicolay Grevstad dated December 22, 1917, in the Knute Nelson Papers, owned by the Minnesota Historical Society. *Gaa Paa*, a radical Minneapolis weekly, was briefly suppressed, *Minneapolis Tidende*, October 10, 1918.

Caution also marked the response of immigrant organizations to the perils of wartime. In 1917 the Norwegian societies in Chicago and Minneapolis suspended their customary 17th of May festivals, a decision provoking a spirited press controversy. The *bygdelags* significantly curtailed their activities, and cultural societies shifted emphasis from Scandinavian history and literature to war-related topics and themes. Sons of Norway adhered to previously arranged schedules, but the Society added to its program a fund drive for the purchase of ambulances for the armed forces. The shift to English within Lutheran congregations accelerated, and in 1918 the recently organized Norwegian Lutheran Church in America resolved to drop the word "Norwegian" from its name, a decision reversed two years later. Several individuals and organizations, notably the Norwegian-Danish Press Association, disavowed a Nordmanns-Forbundet slogan, "once a Norwegian, always a Norwegian." In replying, spokesmen of the group called attention to a familiar proposition now obscured by wartime hysteria: that civic loyalty was one thing and cultural orientation another.[46]

The Norwegian Society of America felt the impact of war to a lesser degree than organizations whose visibility was higher and membership larger. Nor did censorship hamper *Kvartalskrift*, which by definition was a cultural, not a political, journal. However, cultural writings are at times loaded with far-reaching political implications, a reality strikingly illustrated by Ager's five-installment essay, *"Den store udjævning"* (The Great Leveling). Basically the essay is a protest against the pressures for standardization and conformity generated by antihyphenism and significantly strengthened by the war and its aftermath. The first installment appeared in July, 1917, early in the war; the last in *Kvartalskrift's* final issue in 1922, two years after the Red Scare had subsided. Thus the work is more in the nature of an ongoing commentary on an evolving issue rather than on a systematic disquisition, although a consistent frame of reference links the five installments. The whole is not greater than the sum of the parts — quite the contrary. Each of the installments is in fact an essay in its own right,

---

[46] *Normanden*, February 27, March 9, 13, 20, 23, 1917; *Fram*, May 17, 1917; *Reform*, February 27, 1917; Lovoll, *A Folk Epic*, 132–140. On Sons of Norway during the war, see *Minneapolis Tidende*, June 7, 1917, July 25, 1918, April 10, 1919. See also Carl H. Chrislock, "Name Change and the Church, 1918–1920," in *Norwegian-American Studies*, 27: 194–223. *Reform*, September 6, 1918, carried a report of the Norwegian-Danish Press Association meeting. See also *Minneapolis Tidende*, August 15, 1918, and *Normanden*, September 6, 21, 1918.

which can be read independently of the others, and the qualitative range is considerable.

"The Great Leveling" on page 101, a translation of the first installment of the series, analyzes the cultural impact of antihyphenism's leveling tendencies. Diversity of life style, a value highly prized by Americans, was being replaced by a dull, bland, mechanized uniformity. The liquidation of ethnic heritages (a modern writer might use the word "ethnicity") was drying up the only dependable source of creativity, thereby destroying hopes of cultural achievement. American literature was a worthy product, but its merit was primarily attributable to the firm grip of Anglo-American writers on their English heritage.

The third installment, "The Citizen and the State," on page 117, published in 1919, is an excursion into political and constitutional theory. The state, Ager acknowledges, "has the right to demand a great deal" — its "jurisdiction over material goods is unlimited." But it "has absolutely no right to interfere with such concerns . . . as love of parents [and] cultural tastes and preferences." Nor can it compel belief in the rightness of a particular public policy. In the late war, government could appropriately demand that Socialists, pacifists, and pro-Germans "discharge their civic duties." On the other hand, "It had no right . . . to demand an accounting of their inner convictions." If these propositions appear self-evident in the 1970s, they scarcely reflect the prevailing national consensus in 1919. They do, however, reflect the frustration of a dedicated cultural pluralist in the immediate aftermath of the war to make the world safe for democracy.

Formal termination of the war bloodletting on November 11, 1918, did not lift the suspicion which for more than four years had shadowed "hyphenate" America. Quite the contrary. In 1919 two antihyphenist tenets gained widespread popular acceptance: (1) the notion that "foreigners" were a dangerous source of radical infection; and (2) the theory that English was peculiarly the "language of liberty." Proposals aimed at non-English journalism, foreign-language instruction, and "alien" political activity crowded the calendars of most state legislative sessions. In Washington, D.C., demands for drastic restrictions on immigration grew more insistent, and throughout the country "Red" hunting became a major preoccupation.[47]

[47] Higham, *Strangers in the Land*, 254–263.

Obviously such a climate did not encourage a resumption of ethnic activity. Nevertheless, the defeat of Germany reduced pressure sufficiently to permit a degree of ethnic assertiveness. Full-scale 17th of May festivals and well-attended *bygdelag* rallies reemerged; both at times provided the occasion for protests against the "new nativism." The Norwegian-language press also reacted against the excesses of the Americanization crusade more aggressively than during the war. Within Norwegian Lutheran congregations the trend toward English, so pronounced in 1917–1918, temporarily shifted in favor of Norwegian. And in 1920 the Norwegian Lutheran Church in America reversed the 1918 name-change decision, an action which seemed to symbolize the recovery of some of the ground lost during the war.

The early 1920s did in fact witness a recovery, but one that was partial, spotty, and in some sectors temporary. After staging an impressive "last rally," the *bygdelag* movement lost its elan. Thanks to an efficiently managed insurance program, Sons of Norway flourished and prospered. The immigrants' link with Norway had a lower priority than earlier, but sufficient enthusiasm remained to sustain Nordmanns-Forbundet. Although the impressive music festivals of prewar days were not revived, choral and singing societies retained a substantial following. On the other hand, the Norwegian-American press was a declining institution. In 1910 the weekly edition of *Skandinaven* of Chicago served 50,000 subscribers; by 1925 its circulation had shrunk to 25,000. The weekly *Minneapolis Tidende* experienced a comparable decrease: from 32,931 in 1910 to 17,000 in 1925. Although a few papers, notably *Decorah-Posten*, defied the trend for a few years, the demise of Norwegian-American journalism was predictable.[48]

The Norwegian Lutheran church of the 1920s was scarcely a declining institution, but its ethnic role was rapidly diminishing. Two main factors facilitated the trend: (1) closer co-operation with non-Norwegian Lutherans through such organizations as the National Lutheran Council; and (2) an accelerating shift to English which in 1920 reversed the temporary turnabout of the preceding year. The drift profoundly disturbed friends of *norskdommen* both inside and outside the church. "Until a few years ago," wrote Ager in 1922, "the Norwegian church in America was the biggest and most important factor working for preservation of the Norwegian language." He added that

[48] Lovoll, *A Folk Epic*, 140–141, 145–196; Lovoll, "*Decorah-Posten:* The Story of an Immigrant Newspaper," in *Norwegian-American Studies*, 27: 93–94.

he had purposely refrained from also saying "preservation of *norskdommen*" although "this to some extent followed." Since early settlement days, he continued, the Norwegian congregational school had provided the American-born children of immigrants with rudimentary instruction in the Norwegian language and Norwegian culture. This instruction had enhanced rather than impaired the performance of Norwegian-American youth in public-school disciplines, contemporary educational theory notwithstanding. In the five years prior to 1922, maintenance of the Norwegian congregational school had seemed to be an impossibility; in the preceding sixty years, it had not even appeared difficult.[49]

The point was well taken. For two generations or more, the Norwegian congregational school had been the mainstay of elementary instruction in Norwegian. Moreover, the orientation of the church had implications for its academies and colleges, most of which were deemphasizing and curtailing their Norwegian-language programs. Nor was public education in a position to fill the gap. Firmly established programs of Scandinavian studies on the university level survived the war, a few high schools maintained offerings in Norwegian and Swedish, and the Sigvald Quale declamation contests continued — but the prewar campaign to expand Scandinavian studies could not be revived. In elementary schools the limited opportunities for instruction in foreign languages created by statutes such as the Minnesota law of 1907 were removed. By 1920 most states specified that English alone should serve as the medium of instruction in all elementary schools, and Nebraska prohibited all formal foreign-language instruction to students who had not completed the eighth grade.[50]

Given the adverse climate of the time, it is paradoxical that Norwegian-American fiction reached a high level of productivity — perhaps its highest — in the 1920s. As is well known, the recognition of O. E. Rølvaag's literary success peaked during that decade. The first volume of his famous trilogy appeared in 1924, the last in 1931. The works of such writers as Ager, Simon Johnson, Jon Norstog, and Wist — who along with several other authors published in the 1920s — are part of America's "lost literature" produced by ethnic writers. In reflecting on the paradox of high productivity in a time of

---

[49] *Kvartalskrift*, 17–18: 5 (1921–1922).
[50] The United States Supreme Court ultimately declared the Nebraska law unconstitutional. See *Meyer* v *Nebraska*, 262 U.S. 390 (1923).

adversity, one may detect a tragic confluence of forces: at the moment when Norwegian-American culture had achieved the capability of producing a literature worthy of the name, high-pressure assimilation and accelerating urbanization were dissolving that sine qua non of any culture, the communal bond. Ironically, this tragic confluence may have served as a spur to creativity in its own right. In probing the sources of Rølvaag's inspiration, Neil T. Eckstein raises the question of whether the trauma of the war and its aftermath may not have "helped to awaken within Rølvaag the soul of the true artist and to sharpen his perspicacity as a critic." Perhaps the same question can be raised with respect to several other Norwegian-American authors.[51]

In any case, circumstances did not favor a prolonged flowering of Norwegian-American fiction. If Ager's contention that lack of intimate rapport between the writer and a Norwegian-American audience had been a problem in 1914 is correct, the situation was more serious in the 1920s. Fewer and fewer Norwegian Americans retained the capacity and inclination to read the Norwegian language. The competing lure of those harbingers of America's consumer culture, network radio and the cinema, created further difficulty. Moreover, many Norwegian-American readers resented Rølvaag's realistic portrayal of the brutal and coarse aspects of immigrant life in America. Fortunately for him, a wider audience appreciated the merit of his work in translation, thereby guaranteeing recognition of his talent. The other writers were less fortunate.

The success of the 1925 festival commemorating the centennial of the first organized migration from Norway to the United States suggests another paradox. If Norse ethnicity was indeed fading, how could such an impressive spectacle be staged in 1925? A superficial comparison of this event and the 1914 observance of the Eidsvoll Constitution might lead to the conclusion that 1925 was a repeat performance on a larger scale. However, there were marked differences between the two, some obvious and others more subtle — and herein is the key to the paradox. For one thing, the English language predominated in 1925, although Norwegian still held a prominent role in the religious services and presumably in much of the informal socializing. For another, assimilationist rhetoric, while not totally absent in 1914,

[51] Neil T. Eckstein, "O. E. Rølvaag: The Marginality of the Bi-Cultural Writer," in *Ole Rølvaag: Artist and Cultural Leader*, 67. Papers presented at the Rølvaag Symposium held at St. Olaf College, October 28–29, 1974, edited by Gerald Thorson.

was considerably more pronounced in 1925. One may safely say that the Norwegian Americans who celebrated in 1914 did so as Norwegian Americans and were accepted as such by their neighbors. On the other hand, those active in 1925 combined a proclamation of their full emergence as "100 per cent Americans" with a retrospective and nostalgic look at their Norwegian and Norwegian-American past.[52]

At least one prominent Norwegian American refused to capitulate to the spirit of 1925. As in 1914, Waldemar Ager composed an essay for the occasion, a short piece titled *"Omkring hundreaarsfesten"* (Concerning the Centennial Festival) printed in the souvenir program. The contrast between Ager's essay and those of the other contributors is striking. Ager wrote in Norwegian; the others in English. Explicitly or implicitly, the latter accept assimilation as an inevitable and beneficent process; Ager reiterates most of his old complaints against the "now dominant melting pot." Significantly, he omits any reference to the prospects of Norwegian-American literature; presumably he had abandoned hope that it would emerge. Nevertheless, retention of the ethnic heritage was a necessary precondition for any useful Norse contribution to American society. Moreover, knowledge of the experience of one's own group would facilitate understanding the plight of all immigrant groups and in turn contribute to that climate of mutual trust and confidence upon which the nation's security ultimately depended. This notion may seem commonplace, but it was appropriate enough in 1925 when millions of Americans were under the spell of a powerful Ku Klux Klan.[53]

---

[52] Carl H. Chrislock, "The First Two Centennials 1914 and 1925," in *Commemorative Publication of the Norwegian-American Sesquicentennial Association*, 36–37 (Minneapolis, 1975). See also Olaf M. Norlie, *History of the Norwegian People in America*, 302–303 (Minneapolis, 1925).

[53] *Norse-American Centennial, 1825–1925*, 12–13 (Minneapolis, 1925).

II

Our Cultural Stage

by Johs. B. Wist

TRANSLATED BY SIGVALD STOYLEN

IN SPITE of individual expressions in our newspapers and other media about the possibility of a future Golden Age for Norwegian-American literature, apparently it may be taken for granted that most of those who participate in our Norwegian endeavors in this land — and for whom culture and feeling of nationality is something more than the sounding of sonorous chimes or tinkling bells — mainly agree that, in our period of transition as Norwegian Americans, we lack several criteria to be able to stand on our own feet — culturally speaking. The interesting circumstance that we have organized a Norwegian Society among us is in itself an admission that under our peculiar conditions it has been necessary to draw on other cultural sources. In reality, we thereby acknowledge that we are obliged to live off the cultural fruits which already lie ripe and ready for us in literature and history and in our national life and tradition.

It is quite easy to understand that it cannot very well be otherwise,

NOTE. Under the title "Vor kulturelle stilling," this essay appeared in *Kvartalskrift*, 1–10, January, 1905. From 1900 to 1923, Wist edited *Decorah-Posten*, a distinguished immigrant newspaper published in Decorah, Iowa.

since conditions under which we live are not by any means permanent, but only temporary. A transition such as the one Norwegian Americans experience has never been conducive to an independent cultural development, and if we imagine the possibility that our people here should be able to accomplish such a task, we must also think of the possibility that it has become our lot to achieve something that has no parallel in history.

Culturally, we are a people wandering, nomads in transition from one nation to another. As yet we have not by any means reached the fork in the road which of necessity must point the way. Therefore, we have been neither able nor willing entirely to sever the ties which bind us to the land we left. We still feel the need to be aware of Norwegian culture even though this want is manifested in varying degrees by different individuals according to the conditions of their upbringing or livelihood. Undoubtedly, the same conditions will be valid for a long time to come, in other words until our descendants in the second, third, or fourth generation have become assimilated, and, as an integral part of the nation, can more exclusively nurture themselves on its cultural fruits.

It is the acknowledgment of these ideas, neither more nor less, which has brought into being the organization known under the name, The Norwegian Society of America.

In order to create one's own culture and literature, there must of course be something more than two — or at most three or four — authors who write readable stories on infrequent occasions and a half dozen others who, from time to time, show talent and know how to convey an emotion in a well-turned verse. No doubt we are pleased that there may be found Norwegian-American poems and other literary pieces which can stand comparison with literature created under far more favorable conditions than ours. Here let me — to avoid misunderstandings — add that no one is more genuinely happy over an excellent Norwegian-American book than I. But I must still emphasize that the few well-written books by Norwegians living here are derivatives of another culture different from the one which should especially distinguish us as Norwegian Americans. This is also one of the reasons that, no matter how superior these books may be, they represent very little which for us is a peculiarly typical cultural entity. If one may find error in this, the error does not lie with the authors but in the reality of conditions.

The famous American author William Dean Howells has recently declared that as yet not a single truly American novel has been written, and that certainly a long time will pass before such a one emerges. According to his opinion, the national setting as a whole has not yet developed anything culturally typical which could be mirrored in the country's literature. He means something distinctly marked as especially American, which characterizes the original or independent life of the people here in contrast to those of other lands.

By this, Howells does not necessarily mean that there aren't American authors and intellectuals who hold an honored place in literature. No less does he mean that among them are none who, with sufficient emphasis, have indicated their position as American inasmuch as they — with considerable ingenuity and geniality — have described certain provincial aspects of American life and environment. For example, he does not mean that Mark Twain is not an original American humorist or that "The Jumping Frog" is not a genuine provincial product. Neither does he desire to insinuate that authors like Poe, Longfellow, Bryant, or Lowell have not benefited the aesthetic literary milieu of this country.

When he states that no typical American novel has been written, he has pointed out that the novel is the creative form in which a genuine national life first and most fully originates, and he has thus concluded that the representative type is only in the beginning of its future development. Apparently, we believe we can discern its tendencies, but it does not as yet appear as a finished cultural product. This is rather easy to explain. American society has not as yet quite digested the various elements which immigration has contributed. The American people have created a new nation. There are more generative forces available here than perhaps can be matched by any other people, but these forces have not fused together to become a composite whole; and it will take time before this will occur. Thus the material of the typical novel is as yet not present. The original, both in life and literature, is in a high degree provincial, as for example in New England.

There is no American novel which so intensely depicts the life which is distinctly American, as do Bjørnson's descriptions of Norwegian folkways in his peasant novels or Jonas Lie's in his narratives of the sea — just to mention a couple of well-known writers.[1]

---

[1] Bjørnstjerne Bjørnson (1832–1910), Norwegian poet, dramatist, novelist, and social reformer. Jonas Lie (1833–1908), Norwegian novelist.

One of the American authors, who in his special field manifests unusual originality, Joaquin Miller, has won a great name with his songs of the California Sierras. But his writing isn't a special expression of common American sentiment as compared to Vinje's "Ved Rondane" (Ode to the Mountains), and to other nature poems which both in composition and interpretation are Norwegian.[2] American writings are not like these Norwegian classics saturated by the people's own emotion and perception so that one in every stanza feels the breath of the nation's culture and the awakening from which they have sprung.

To some degree, these examples will serve to illustrate our own Norwegian-American conditions. If America has not yet been able to produce a typical national literature, one perhaps dare not hope that a small Norwegian population — which on the one hand is influenced by its homeland and on the other by America — will be able to create an independent literature or contribute to source material for an original intellectual life which may sufficiently approximate our needs here in this country.

These conditions do not reflect our own Norwegian-American situation in that they cast a shadow over the intellectual endeavors which have been achieved among us. There is no complaint intended here about the accomplishments of our authors, schools, and churches. To the contrary, one must rather admire their work, considering the unfavorable situations which often have prevailed.

The intellectual accommodations which have come into being among us during our period of transition perhaps are due to the influence of the culture of the homeland. Often it has been difficult to make even minor adjustments, but of necessity enough American traits and characteristics have been absorbed by those involved to suit the new environment. An unbiased observer must admit that both school and church have made significant accomplishments.

For this, we are indebted to the leaders of the church and to the distinctly religious character of our people. But, because the interests of the church have been predominant among us, all other intellectual endeavors have become more or less subordinated. The church has utilized all its sources of service, and we don't begrudge the fact that it hasn't educated our young men to become authors, for the people did not ask for authors — they asked for pastors.

I will not here discuss further the influence of the Norwegian-

[2] Aasmund Olafsson Vinje (1818–1870), Norwegian poet.

American free church on Norwegian culture and nationality in America. The men of the church, without any harmful effects, certainly could have maintained a livelier communication with the homeland than they have done. Personally, however, I have become more and more convinced that the church has a natural function of leadership among Norwegians in this land. I also believe for two reasons that this was the best that could happen: (1) because of the overwhelming importance that the Lutheran faith through the church should become transplanted from parents to children and future generations, and (2) because it and *it alone* could satisfy the all-important spiritual need which occupied our people in the beginning. This condition has given the church a natural privilege, which it is right and correct that it should have. It also follows that all cultural and national endeavors among us must be placed in a setting conducive to elicit sympathy and co-operation from the men of the church, if their efforts are to come to fruition.

It is self-evident that for the church its own particular needs are most important, but of course from this it does not follow that everything else is irrelevant. The opposite is true; our clergymen, along with our Norwegian schools and newspapers, in addition to church work, have engaged in significant cultural pursuits by strengthening interest in the Norwegian language. In other ways they have also been mighty supporters of Norwegian attainments among us. But in spite of these facts, one must still maintain that these and similar activities are calculated to alleviate temporary spiritual exigencies. Culturally speaking, this influence of the church has succeeded, depending more or less on whether one has catered to Norwegian or American interests or to Norwegian or American culture.

Thus our people stand in transition and are influenced by both cultures. What elements of the Norwegian heritage we brought along depend on the participation which our lot in life has afforded us. In addition, we carry with us Norwegian characteristics infusing new ways and conditions. We are all to some extent conscious of nationality, although we are not all alike, and it becomes difficult to discard the influences that Norwegian tradition holds over us. If we were left to ourselves, we no doubt would foster and further develop our ethnic characteristics, a forward step which in time would produce an independent culture and literature.

But we are not so fortunate as to be left to ourselves. On the contrary, we always feel how the American society, which we have found here all about us and to which we as loyal citizens owe all, draws us to itself closer and closer. As opportunities occur, we learn its language, read its papers, and become acquainted with its literature. We also participate in its public life according to our abilities and circumstances. And, just as we become more closely bound to the soil which nourishes us, so we become more and more involved in the affairs of the country for which we feel responsibilities as participants. While we still consider ourselves as Norwegians — and of course in reality we cannot be anything else — we soon notice another force making its presence felt, of which we were previously unaware. If this is true for the immigrant, it is of course more so for his children, who do not know any other country than America. For them, what especially distinguishes their parents as Norwegians, even under the best of conditions, has become watered down, while what draws our people and all other immigrant groups closer to American ways has gained the upper hand.

Those interests which do not have ties to the fatherland and do not involve church activities become absorbed by the society in which we will and must become useful members. What the immigrants have brought along as their heritage is not sufficient for present or future needs. We must therefore be in a position to relate to both Norwegian and American intellectual life, so that from one of these sources or both we can gain the sustenance we need to live a cultured life. This holds for literature and also for other factors included in the concept of enlightenment. What we ourselves can create in literary pursuits can be a goal for the varied interests which occupy us in our period of transition. Rightly, however, it would be unfair to call this goal a cultural measurement; if that should be the criterion, we would not have much to brag about and still less to build on. In this regard, like other transitional groups, we share certain weaknesses. We feel that we possess power and believe that with a solid economic base we can accomplish almost anything. But there are sufficient tasks to tackle without trying to lift something which the laws of gravity forbid. And under conditions like ours, as previously stated, neither the Norwegians nor any other people have succeeded in creating an independent literature, even though they must have influenced the prevailing culture in the countries in which they settled.

It can truly be said that Iceland is the only example proving that an independent Norwegian literature can originate and thrive outside Norway. But to infer from this that something similar can be repeated in this country is — to use a mild expression — a rather daring conclusion. Since Iceland was exclusively inhabited by Norsemen, naturally no culture or literature not of Norwegian origin could develop. When the Norsemen settled in Iceland, they brought their heritage along, and there was none other that could compete. Through the centuries, there was a luxurious flowering of literature in Iceland, and the Norwegian culture with deep roots in the Viking Age grew faster there in song and saga than it did in Norway. But times have changed. We did not come to this country as masters or conquerors; we came as poor immigrants with the goal of making a better life. A large civilized society stood ready and prepared to receive us — to assimilate us.

Most of us have accepted the fact that our children — and of necessity our children's children — will feel bound to this country's culture and will regard it as their own birthright. For us it is perhaps enough to hope that the Norwegian language and nationality will long live in this land and that our endeavors will continue to bear fruit if properly directed. We realize that no Norwegian nor other immigrant group could have dominated American culture; thus we also understand that we cannot transmit intact our Norwegian heritage to our immediate descendants.

We all no doubt agree that we should promote and encourage Norwegian-American literary production. If some book appears which reasonably deserves recognition, let us give it due honor. That we as yet cannot create an individual Norwegian-American literature is not a criticism of our authors but only a factual situation. We still depend on the fatherland and its literature; we simply cannot be without the nurture which Norwegian culture provides, until we are ready to embrace what America offers. To declare that we at our present stage can do without the influence of the homeland is the same as declaring ourselves spiritually bankrupt.

The only reason that I have considered these ideas so extensively here is that, according to my opinion, it is extremely important that the Norwegian Society from the very beginning should decide its present aim and future task: the necessity to foster communication with Norwegian culture. I wish to avoid every suspicion that I seek to attack any of our authors, their poems or other works. They have written much that deserves more than passing notice, even though there certainly is considerable chaff among the wheat. What has been written here in some measure will serve to clarify apprehensions, not to be taken lightly, that — for some here and there — unpleasant truths have been expressed.

The Norwegian Society according to its program is obligated to build bridges and maintain the bridges which already exist between the fatherland and its emigrated children. This is self-evident. Thank God it is a mistaken idea that there is no headland to which the other end of the bridge can be fastened. There are hundreds of these!

III

Our Cultural Possibilities

by Waldemar Ager

TRANSLATED BY SIGVALD STOYLEN

T HE first number of *Kvartalskrift* included a suitable essay about our cultural stage by Johs. B. Wist.
 Without wanting to involve myself in direct refutation of possibly correct, commonly held views, there are, nevertheless, other opinions which deserve consideration. I do not know of any other subject of more importance than the preceding one involving the Norwegian Society and its aims. As a practical matter, should the Society mainly stress the greater influence of Norwegian culture upon Norwegian Americans and encourage that direction, or should it stress and promote further interest in a special Norwegian-American culture and heritage? Either course will implement the other. If one succeeds, so will the other. But before that can happen, we have to have faith in our own potentialities. The purpose of this plea is only to strengthen such a belief.
 It is necessary for us to try to create something ourselves. An immigrant heritage which only exists in its ability to continue to nur-

NOTE. This article, under the title "Vore kulturelle muligheter," was published in *Kvartalskrift*, 2–10, April, 1905.

ture itself on Norwegian culture is unthinkable. If a culture deserves the name of culture, it must contribute, create something. If Norwegian influence really is worthwhile and to some degree takes hold here, it will bear fruit, some of which we must be prepared to accept and harvest. If, for instance, we have faith that we can awaken a greater appreciation for Norwegian literature, then we must conclude that its inspiring sources should be utilized. We must prepare the ground for the development which such literature will bring forth. Otherwise it isn't of much use.

There are other reasons. If we admit that we now are in transition from one nation to another, then our saga will only be written in a way to indicate that we have left independent cultural traces which mirror our own lives, our own struggles. We know full well that ethnic groups in this country have become completely assimilated without leaving their cultural traces, but we also acknowledge that this is sad indeed and of little honor to their nationality.

Suppose that there could be created a market here for Norwegian-American literature. At first perhaps the potential products would be met with scorn and shrugs on the part of knowledgeable critics among our kinsmen across the sea. But most of the few attempts which have been made have met with the approval of our own people. If a successful production of readable books could just be created here, then the interest in Norwegian literature would follow as surely as the piano has replaced the organ in affluent homes.

There are great difficulties in creating an interest in modern Norwegian literature among our people. We are not at the same stage of development as our relatives across the ocean. The whole stirring period in Norwegian literature from *Synnøve* to *Trætte mænd* (Weary Men) is one of emptiness here.[1] Speaking in a literary sense, we belong to the age of Hans Nielsen Hauge.[2] Modern Norwegian literature is an empty book for the greater part of our people. Not because it is inaccessible, but because in the mass we lack the comprehension to understand and appreciate it. Much is being read especially by the farmers, but they read newspapers, devotional or religious tracts about

---

[1] *Synnøve Solbakken*, a romantic peasant tale by Bjørnstjerne Bjørnson, published in 1857. *Weary Men*, a novel by Arne Garborg published in 1891, describes the decadence of the times.

[2] Hans Nielsen Hauge (1771–1824), lay preacher and popular educator whose activities generated a major religious revival in Norway. His strongly Puritan followers were known as Haugeans.

predestination before they choose Bjørnson, Ibsen, or Hamsun.[3] They find in their papers and tracts a culture which relates to something in their own background.

There are few of us who have lived the greater part of our lives here who can particularly benefit from *Lille Eyolf* (Little Eyolf), *Når vi døde vågner* (When We Dead Awaken), and other recent works by the great Norwegian authors.[4] They are as strange to us as is American literature. It is not so much a question of artistic content as it is of what we, at our present stage, can digest. A man for instance wishes to arouse appreciation for music in a settlement where there is little or no interest in it. He can attract the world's greatest virtuosos and let them play for the people for little or nothing to awaken their appreciation for music in this manner. Or he can encourage people to obtain instruments to begin to develop whatever talent is present within their own circle. I believe the latter would be the most sensible if it is development that they seek.

One must have acquired a considerable musical taste to enjoy and profit from the works of a master. I am disposed to believe that it is just as hopeless to transplant any greater part of Norwegian culture in Norwegian-American soil as it would be to develop a real culture here in America. I believe that the one is as easy as the other.

What really stands in the way of a sprouting of literature among us? History does not deny the possibility. If the *Edda* songs originated among Norsemen who lived in England, it may be proof that literature of a high order can grow under conditions which in some degree remind us of our own. Regarding this particular matter, however, history carries little weight. We have the telegraph, railroads, steamships, and above all newspapers. Intellectually speaking, Norwegians in Minneapolis are closer to our fatherland today than the Norwegian Society in Copenhagen was a hundred years ago.[5]

Peer O. Strømme and Wilhelm Pettersen are considerably more Norwegian than Ludvig Holberg and Johan Herman Wessel, who lived in Denmark.[6] Most of the great Norwegian literary works came into

---

[3] Henrik Ibsen (1828–1906), famous Norwegian dramatist and poet. Knut Hamsun (1859–1952), Norwegian novelist.

[4] *Little Eyolf*, dramatic play by Henrik Ibsen published in 1894. *When We Dead Awaken*, a drama published in 1899, concluding Ibsen's writing in that field.

[5] The Norwegian Society in Copenhagen came into being among Norwegian academicians at the University of Copenhagen in 1772. It became the hearth of Norwegian national culture during these years.

[6] Peer O. Strømme (1856–1921), Norwegian-American minister, lecturer, novelist,

being in foreign lands; so the influence of a foreign people may be figured as an advantage. That the national character in this country has not conditioned itself to become entirely typical and that it does not offer material for the literature of folkways as in the European countries may be true enough. But it is only one branch of literature which deals with this point. Most of Ibsen's characters aren't especially Norwegian. His pastor "Brand" and Hall Caine's pastor "John Strong" seem to be cast in the same mold.[7] Furthermore it is a question whether we don't here have character types which are singularly Norwegian-American. As an example, consider the delightful "Klemetsrud" in *Hvorledes Halvor blev prest* (How Halvor Became a Minister).[8] Klemetsrud is well known by readers of our time in America, but Norwegian literature does not know him. What couldn't the theater create with such a character? Surely there is sufficient material for poets and authors in this country.

In this issue of *Kvartalskrift* is a narrative of a settlement in Goodhue County, Minnesota. One would have to be both deaf and blind if he could not see subjects in such characters as the Talla brothers, Storesvein, Halvor "the devil," and the like. Such persons in the course of time become sources for talented authors to write about. That conclusion cannot be avoided. How much material doesn't old "Kaskeland" [Koshkonong] hide? When the time is ripe, when such material begets authorship, there will be no need for urging our people to read books.

Objections are raised about language difficulties. It will only be a short period that Norwegian will continue to survive in this country, it is said. Maybe so. But the same was said more vehemently twenty, thirty years ago. In the countryside the Norwegian language persists into the third generation. In some ways, we are more Norwegian here than they are in Norway. The middle and upper classes there are mixed considerably with other nationals. The many foreign names indicate this fact. The mass of Norwegian immigrants was almost exclusively made up of peasants. Proportionally, there are more typical

---

newspaper correspondent, and world traveler. Wilhelm Pettersen (1860–1932), Norwegian-American educator and poet. Ludvig Holberg (1684–1754), Norwegian-Danish dramatist and historian. He is considered the father of modern literature in Norway and Denmark. Johan Herman Wessel (1742–1785), Norwegian-Danish poet active in the Norwegian Society in Copenhagen.

[7] Hall Caine (1853–1931), English novelist.
[8] *How Halvor Became a Minister*, a novel by Peer O. Strømme.

Norwegian names among the professors at our higher educational institutions here than in Norway's university.

One thing is absolutely certain. There are higher institutions in Norway where the ideals of culture show the influence of German and French models. The Norwegian schools in this country have their ideals in Norway and in what is typically Norwegian. The Norwegian church here has been less exposed to foreign influence than has the state church of Norway.

The people of Swedish descent living in Finland must have been less favorably situated than we are. In a way, they had to struggle with three languages, of which both Finnish and Russian actually had a greater justification than Swedish. It was more difficult for them to seek sustenance from Swedish than it is for us to seek nurture in Norway's culture. Proportionally, their number was also insignificant. However, they fostered names like Runeberg and Topelius. They were perhaps in a way Swedish, but their writings involved the Finnish people and Finnish nature. It can hardly be said that they were pupils of their kinsmen across the Baltic. The main point is that these Swedish immigrants preserved the language and the love for the roots from which they had sprung. It can readily be admitted that it is difficult to "live" in two languages and have two "fatherlands," if one may say so. But, properly utilized, this difficulty can even be an advantage. George du Maurier had been educated in an English home in France and hardly knew which country he belonged to most.[9] In his three books, one can feel how both countries and both languages left their stamp on him. If I recollect correctly he wrote *Peter Ibbetson* both in English and French. The excellence of his English is acknowledged by all. Yes, many read his books only for the sake of their language.

It is most important to preserve interest in the Norwegian language. It seems as if it takes many generations for a people to "learn" a language. The Norse literature deteriorated when Danish penetrated Norway. And to this day, the Norwegians struggle under the feeling that they have not as yet learned the Danish language — even as closely related as it is — sufficiently to get along with that alone. During the time of this penetration, it was "proper" in Denmark to

---

[9] Johan Ludvig Runeberg (1804–1877), Finnish poet whose outstanding work *Songs of Ensign Stål*, 1848, represents a treasure house of Finnish patriotic inspiration. Zacharias Topelius (1818–1898), Finnish writer and historian. Both Topelius and Runeberg used the Swedish language. George du Maurier (1834–1896), English novelist and illustrator.

write and talk only Latin, German, or French. So nothing of literary importance appeared in spite of the flowering of literature in other lands. Before Holberg's time, it was considered more "inferior" to write books in Danish than it is for us here to write books in Norwegian. And there was no lack of learned men who were fully conversant with the European cultural languages.

Holberg wrote what he perhaps considered his masterwork, *Niels Klim*, in Latin, and surrendered it to oblivion, although he had marked it for eternity. We must, however, still keep the mother tongue, unwise as this may seem, even though we have a world language like English at our disposal. For a people to give up their own language is tantamount to decay. It is not only the "words" that are lost. We can lose our Norwegian language by letting it slip away. We can keep it and let our children learn it as long as we ourselves wish. There is no invariable judgment hanging over us in that connection, as some seem to think. It seems more to the point that knowledge of both languages is a great advantage. Many Norwegians born and educated here speak the old language excellently. The Norwegian newspapers which are edited by Norwegians born here rank linguistically above, rather than below, those edited by Norwegian immigrants.

The conditions in which a literature can grow here are not as unfavorable as many believe. We have just as many readers as there were in all of Norway in Wergeland's time. And the ability to buy is much greater. That books of any importance have not been published is due to several causes. Great writing does not appear spontaneously. Homes, churches, schools had to be built first. Norway hasn't much to show either from 1807 to 1830. Great religious movements stirred the country. After independence from Denmark was achieved in 1814, education and politics occupied people's minds. When finally real indications of a Norwegian literary creativity appeared, the critics measured it by Danish standards and condemned it to death, saying that for a long time the country would have to nourish itself on Danish culture.

The Norwegian people have made tremendous progress while they have lived and built here. The first and most necessary tasks have been partly accomplished. If our schools continue to thrive and grow, we can be prepared for a surplus of intellectual energy and activity in the future. There will be a need for Norwegian books. Up to the present, we haven't done much to satisfy this need. The accusation has been made that stories of crime, published by Waldemar Kriedt's company in Minneapolis, are the most widely read books here. That is not because they are cheaper than other books, but because they relate to our people, who to a great extent lack qualifications to appreciate modern Norwegian fiction.

It certainly is very strange if there aren't any geniuses among the million Norwegians in this country, while there is such a surplus in Norway. Perhaps they just wait for opportunities to blossom forth to do great deeds. As it is now, no one seems to have any faith in this judgment, and when there is no encouragement great achievements won't materialize.

I once saw a farm boy sitting by a counter in a store in a small town in Lac qui Parle County in Minnesota; he was drawing pictures with a pencil. With a few lines he sketched the faces of those present. Anyone who knows anything about drawing knows that a boy without any education cannot do this without considerable talent. But the boy's big dream was to get to Minneapolis to learn to draw crayon portraits.

A young man born in North Dakota, who was quite a master on the violin, cornet, and piano, had the ambition to learn as many instruments as possible and to become a leader of a brass band. I only mention these examples to indicate how talents become diverted among a people who believe that they have no native ability.

There was once a belief that pastors had to be brought from Norway if they were to amount to anything. The church needed literature and it attained it. The temperance people needed literature in their crusade, and what they have accomplished compares favorably with what has been done in Norway. A self-made painter in our town has exhibited a painting of a woodland scene as beautiful as anyone could wish. The air lies clear and cold among the trees which the ax has cut down. The snow delicately covers stumps and tufts, and so the scene is a joy to behold. But in the middle of the road appears a large load of timbers as if to be photographed, the most rounded and even logs which would please the eyes of a lumberjack. The chains, the harness, the newly painted sled, the powerful draft horses — the whole procession is almost painfully realistic, as if the value of the painting were dependent on the solidity of the logs or the proper loading.

We get a somewhat similar impression of the literature we have here, but the background often tells us what it could have become. A cultural development among our people could hardly have manifested itself in any different way. The first immigrants followed the same footsteps as the Norwegian people did after their country's separation from Denmark. Work, religious movements, and politics engaged them wholly. Homes, churches, and schools had to be built. Now for the most part these have been finished. Other interests will arise. The organ or the piano are among the last arrivals on the farm. Later there will be a call for paintings and other works of art. Every prosperous Norwegian farm will have a book case, and there will be those who will love fiction and the collecting of books.

But in order to create a book market, we must have faith in it. As it is now we will bury a real author as soon as his head appears. Our best men point over the ocean to Norway, like those in Wergeland's time who pointed to Denmark.[10] Our first Norwegian-American author will have to be very tolerant, but he will come — and perhaps we won't know him when he does come. Most of those who have written books have peddled them themselves, and seldom have they been able to afford to write more than one. In Norway people won't recognize a Norwegian-American author, and likewise I am tempted to say we won't here either.

Our musicians are in the same fix. When Olive Fremstad appeared in our midst as a singer of first rank, our own Norwegian papers could not give reliable information about her.[11] She speaks Norwegian and considers herself a Norwegian. Finally when Hanna Larsen in San Francisco interviewed her a few weeks ago, she could report that Miss Fremstad felt hurt that her own countrymen were the last to accord recognition.[12] A Norwegian-American musician has to be a magnificent genius to cope with a fourth- or fifth-class fiddler in Norway.

We had need for pastors and men like Gjermund Hoyme, and the many prominent names in our Lutheran church records bear witness to their work.[13] We needed businessmen and we got them. We had need of politicians and they appeared — giants among them. We needed speakers to lecture, and many of them in their field can be compared to

[10] Henrik Wergeland (1808–1845), Norwegian poet who advocated an artistic independence for Norway.
[11] Olive Fremstad (1870–1951), Norwegian-American opera singer. She performed at the Metropolitan Opera in New York from 1903 to 1914, and was especially successful in Wagnerian roles.
[12] Hanna Larsen was editor of the Norwegian-American newspaper *Pacific-Posten* in San Francisco.
[13] Gjermund Hoyme (1847–1902), Norwegian-American church leader. He was president of the Conference, 1886–1890, and of the United Lutheran Church, 1890–1902.

what our old fatherland has to offer. Should it be impossible to obtain authors, painters, musicians, sculptors if it really became clear to us that we have need of them? Not if our Norwegian schools for instance would show more interest — and also the newspapers.

It is not my purpose here to refute Mr. Wist's excellent article. I wish only to consider the other side of the question, as I previously stated. The one side does not exclude the other. Just the opposite. The one will necessarily attract the other.

asserted itself to a greater degree in the fields of art and industry than it appears to have done — assuming that everything had turned out as the older people expected.

Those who were born here have the advantage of knowledge of the language and of local conditions. They were freed from the struggle for food which their parents had endured when they came here — poor and often to be the subject of ridicule. In spite of the fact that the young do well in school and that in most cases they have become more or less "Yankeefied," the "greenhorns" who came over a few years ago have gone ahead of them. It is these older people who have entered the legislatures and businesses and gained repute and prosperity. How did this come about? Yes, perhaps in order to progress in the world, among the best qualifications needed must be included something called "character."

What is it? How is character formed? It cannot be bought, cannot be made factory-like in the schools. When a house is built, a strong foundation is needed as well as good materials, soundly and fittingly put into place. It is not sufficient that the foundation be substantial if the materials are poor. Neither is it sufficient that both foundation and materials be good if the construction is not solidly and appropriately fitted together.

A character is not a single virtue or a single peculiarity, but several suited and joined on a firm base to result in a harmonious whole. One cannot form character by orders or recipes from cookbooks. It must have its deep origin in the child's inborn ability to attach itself to its own family and to its race. The education and the heritage which parents can give a child ought to stress that it should feel related to this larger family. And it must then become a further extension of its own racial inheritance.

To form a character which is worth much in life's struggle, a fundamental element is required: a mother tongue tied to pride in family and race. The greater part of the Norwegian youth who grow up in this country receive neither the one nor the other. That is the failure and fault of the parents, for no child is born, be it ever so poor, that does not possess a God-given right to a mother tongue accompanied by the love of a fatherland.

Researchers have hardly penetrated deeply enough into the importance of language in a person's spiritual life. One knows that a nation's language is its history and surely that refers back to the country's origin in its misty past. And the words through centuries-long adaptations and additions are naturally better suited to the characteristic dispositions and perceptions of the same race than are those of a hastily acquired language. When all is said, there is for each individual only one language which can reach the inner recesses of the mind — and that is the mother tongue.

A Norwegian sailor tells about a fire on a big English ship while at sea. As far as one could judge, it looked like certain disaster. As is often the case during such circumstances, several of the crew began to pray to God for salvation. This particular sailor was surprised to find that many prayed in Norwegian, in spite of the fact that for many a Norwegian on board, it was a forgotten or discarded language. And yet under these circumstances, they had only one language in which to express their need — and that was the mother tongue. Until the fire came, the sailor who told the story had believed that he was the only Norwegian on the ship.

Dr. A. Daae, a Norwegian physician in Chicago, relates that he was hurriedly called to a factory where a man had been hurt in a machine accident. The man, a foreman, had been a quiet, reserved, strong person who was thought to be Irish. As the doctor worked over the stricken man, he regained consciousness and made an attempt to fold his hands. His lips moved and one could hear "Our Father, who art in heaven . . ." in Norwegian. Here was another who had never revealed his national origin.

This phenomenon has been observed on battlefields and in hospitals. It is often thus when the wounded or dying face death. The last words from their lips, while the curtain between this life and eternity is being drawn aside, are in a language which neither the doctor nor the nurse understands. "He was a foreigner," "He was a stranger," they say. The last words were in the mother tongue. A good mother's triumph over the whole world. A dying son who had learned the first meaningful speech from her lips dies with these words upon his lips.

And it is the greatest of all when it is a mother's triumph over all evil powers in this world, which perhaps have bewildered the boy. It is then that these last words were the ones which should carry him safely over the waters beyond which his mother perhaps was waiting.

What great thinker is it who has failed to form his thoughts in the mother tongue? Has any preacher or speaker succeeded in stirring inspiration in any other words than those of his own language? And when a great author attempts to set down the most tender emotions on paper, does he then use any other language than his native speech?

The majority of the Norwegian children who grow up here do not acquire a mother tongue. Mother has one; she got that from her mother, but she has a feeling that it is not good enough for her children. The women want "smart" children, and they tell each other proudly that their children do not understand a single word of Norwegian. Not a word — if they want to be really swank. What the women themselves can say is restricted to household words like "Shut your mouth," "Quit that monkey business," and the like. Then comes the day — a bitter day — when the parents discover that they cannot converse intelligently with their own children.

The children leave the home and go into the world without having learned to know their parents. They never got to know the soul of the mother or the heart strings of the father. They could have learned these things through the language — the language of the heart.

Others can — even if they are old and gray — close their eyes and hear their fathers' and mothers' voices after they are departed. One remembers their stories and advice. One really does not have any other storehouse of sustenance to draw upon when the world about threatens evil. We need just such a source of strength in life's struggle. This treasure, this heritage, the poorest mother can give to her son, her daughter. And it is a treasure that neither moth nor rust can destroy. It shall build a wall around the character and protect a younger person when evil days appear.

Under what influence do the smart Norwegian children of the even smarter Norwegian parents grow up? The answer is that of a stammering mother who couldn't make herself sufficiently understood — who couldn't express herself the way she wanted to, because she herself didn't understand the words she used. They were brought up by mother who could not in a motherly way express her words because they often became a hindrance. Such expressions as "What's the matter with you?", "Never mind that," and "Quit that monkey business" are not much to sustain a human soul in life's struggle.

As an example, I once heard a woman use the expression "Shut your mouth" to her little girl, who had interrupted our conversation. When I suggested that such expressions could be said in a nicer way, the mother replied that she did not know any other way to tell the child to be quiet. One may hear Norwegian women use really coarse, rude words in English, only because they do not know their meaning. It is not the language of the heart these mothers speak to their children; it is the language of the street. Such an influence is demoralizing. A person's progress and his character are always shaped by his family relationships.

It is very important that children should have respect for their parents. "Honor thy father and thy mother that thy days may be long upon the land," we learned. I am no theologian, but I am of the opinion that the fourth commandment does not mean that one shall seek to live to a certain old age. Just the opposite — it means that one's reputation shall long endure among his descendants even after one has departed. Consider further not only our father and mother but also our grandfather and grandmother and their parents, in other words those from whom we are sprung — the rock from which we are hewn as the Old Testament expresses it. If we do that, we shall prosper and live long in the land — even in this land. That is my understanding.

It is very natural that you believed that things would go better if you forgot your father and mother and what they represented. And that you believed it was a hindrance for the progress of your children that you should honor your parents by transferring to your own children the heritage your parents bestowed on you. Just as you neglected your parents' heritage and memory, so your children will neglect your memory — neither shall you live long in the land. Or to put it in another way: you shall die and be separated from the lives of your children who remain after you. As much of yourself as you bestowed upon your children, that much of you will live in these children, even if you die. You can feel it long before you die, if you are continuing to live in your children. There are parents who have such a strong feeling that they are living again in their children that they hardly recognize their own advancing years.

Haven't the Americanized Norwegian young people shown a strong tendency to scorn their parents? Not only do they often reject the father's Norwegian name — if he himself has not rejected it — but without the slightest compunction they sell the father's old homestead no matter how much toil has been exerted to create it. For these young people, the childhood home only represents so and so much per acre. The father is dead and often forgotten long before the preacher has thrown three shovels of dirt on him. Has anyone seen any person prosper who despised or did not honor his parents?

How is it possible for the "smart" Norwegian children to honor their even "smarter" parents? Since they do not understand the parents' mother tongue, they can never enter into their parents' thoughts. But they must experience something; so their first impressions are derived from the streets closest to the home. Because of their superior knowledge of the English language, it often becomes the children who lead the parents instead of the parents leading the children. Many parents learn their English from their children, who thus become their teachers. The children learn certain expressions on the streets and pass them on to their parents. The habits of the street penetrate the home. The children get the impression early that they are superior to their parents.

The most pitiful sight I know is that of a father who stammers and struggles to make himself understandable to his own child — like an awkward suitor who is at a loss for words. If the child doesn't get the impression that the father is a dullard, then it is because the child itself has a low mentality. Such childhood experiences do not serve to teach the youngster to honor his parents.

Under proper and natural circumstances, the children during their growing up should learn to understand and become closer to their parents, as naturally as a branch becomes more firmly attached to the trunk of the tree as it grows bigger. Surely among us there seems to be a rule that children and parents grow apart as the years go by. Often when I have given lectures on this subject, I have turned to the women with a question, asking whether they did not themselves feel closer and understand their children better when they were helplessly babbling in their cradles than when they were in their teens and graduating from high school. And silence followed with dejected expressions on many faces. Such women have meant well, but they have not understood the importance of the power of the mother tongue to tie the children to their parents.

One cannot teach children to honor their parents in the way many well-meaning but stupid Norwegian parents raise them. From the time the child is old enough to understand, it learns that food which it does not like is old-country food, outmoded and ugly clothing is old-country style, peculiar people with crooked legs and hunchbacks are old-countrylike, awkward people who say grace at the table are of the old country. Two braids on the back or a patch on the pants are old-country style. To make use of hands, to patch, to darn, to exhibit ridiculous thrift are old-country ways. The quintessence of everything stupid, ill-bred, distasteful, intolerable is so because it exists in the old country. Mother is "peculiar" and in many ways "funny," an acquisition from the old country. Grandmother is even "funnier" and "queerer," for she is even more old-countrylike. That is the child's idea about mother and grandmother. In such a manner it learns to honor them.

And when the children early learn to scorn their parents, it is because something old-country is always attached to them. You may be sure that in just the way you taught your children to make fun of your parents, your offspring will teach their youngsters to make fun of you. The honor you denied your parents will also escape you. When children grow up under these conditions, they draw apart from their parents. Mother gets only the recognition which a waitress expects, and as regards "papa," his children are only interested in what he can earn.

I will note here that we as a race have just as much right to honor the memory of our forefathers who were Norsemen as the New Englanders have to honor their ancestors who were English. I believe the same about the citizens of the Southern states whose forebears were French or Spanish. Hopefully, a man can be just as good a citizen whether he knows one or two languages. We show our loyalty best in educating men and women with character. It is no dependable sign that a man is a good citizen just because he can speak only English.

Feelings of nationality, traditions, race are very important elements in the formation of a character that will leave its imprint. The great reformers like Luther and Melanchthon, authors like Goethe and Schiller, musicians like Mozart and Beethoven, or a philosopher like Kant — all are stamped with peculiarities belonging to the Germans. The great Frenchmen are often characterized by the elegance, geniality and spontaneity which are peculiar to their country. The somber English sense of reality and energy that one finds in Darwin and Newton one also discovers in the dramas of Shakespeare as well as in the sermons of Spurgeon. The glow and color of the Italian do not leave him in Raphael's paintings, Dante's poetry, or Paganini's music.

It seems that Raphael had to be Italian to be Raphael, Luther German to be Luther, Darwin English to be Darwin, and the like.

Their accomplishments were not only determined by their talent but also conditioned by the capacities they had absorbed from the peculiarities and advantages of their race.

And, therefore, many basic qualities are demanded to instill character in a man whether he be insignificant or be held in high regard in the world. The same courage and obstinacy which the Norwegians evidenced in 1814, when they wanted to build an independent state, are just as necessary today in the poor Norwegian who wants to clear a quarter section of land in the forests of Wisconsin or to build himself a future home on the great prairies.

Does it pay then to preserve our identities and traditions as long as they do not conflict with our duties as citizens of this country? I will begin to answer this question by hastening to say that it is only the chosen among nations who have anything to preserve. The old Norsemen well knew that the criterion for living a long life in the land was dependent on honoring their forebears. And they didn't derive this understanding from the catechism. They spoke and sang about the deeds of their fathers, and those who emigrated to Iceland brought along this custom. The result was that a foundation was laid for a literature and culture which few countries can parallel.

So the old generations lived long, and their memory won't die as long as folk live and dwell in Iceland. And they have had great influence. Neither Iceland nor Norway has experienced the subjugation and repression so common in the history of other countries.

V

Proposals for Consideration

by Herman Fjelde

TRANSLATED BY BEN R. EGGAN

AT THE annual meeting of the Norwegian Society, the officials were instructed to send out an appeal to Norwegians in this country, and we shall go to work without evasion.

Our position as immigrants in America, together with that of other races and people, gives us problems to solve that demand attention and a great deal of seriousness. Whether we want a rapid assimilation with these other people or not, the situation in this year of our Lord 1906 is that there exists a kind of Norwegian-American community of close to one million people that is considered to be Norwegian-American. It is regarded as such and will be so reckoned by future historical research. This is a fact that we can determine without further ado.

But once this has come to be regarded as an unalterable fact, then as good citizens we must make an effort to understand our position and

NOTE. This appeal to the members of the Norwegian Society, under the title "Til overveielse og lidt til," was published in *Kvartalskrift*, 2–5, October, 1906. Fjelde, a physician in the Red River Valley of North Dakota, was active in the promotion of Norwegian literary and artistic traditions, and he was responsible for the erection of statues of famous Norwegians. He was the secretary of the Society.

raise our people to the greatest possible heights among the others. Both reason and a sense of honor will grant us this place. We have children who are growing up and it depends on us whether the Norwegian character — which in any case will attach to them — will repress or advance them. It depends on us whether it will be to their honor or to their humiliation that they are of Norwegian ancestry — after we, their parents and grandparents, have gone to rest.

That the social position of the immigrant people in this country is distinctive and very difficult, one will clearly understand from the fact that some immigrant groups develop to success in American surroundings, while others deteriorate. They degenerate under exactly the same exterior conditions that exist for all, the same laws and the same schools and privileges. As far as we know, no one has given a definite reason for this peculiar situation. There is a tendency to take into account average figures of good and bad, but these do not reveal any clear warning to any single group.

We ought to have statistics prepared for our Norwegian people in states where it is possible to do so. We ought to find out about criminality and mental illnesses among our people, for both the first and second generations. We ought to keep ourselves constantly informed and find out whether our people are degenerating from year to year. In that case, we can set things aright and find a remedy more easily than can the American authorities who naturally cannot give individual immigrant groups special attention. In this way, we can perform for our adopted country a considerable service.

Another question is this: Do the parish schools, especially in their instruction in Norwegian and religion, retard our children in the public schools — that is, does the parochial school help or hinder our children's progress? This question has not been answered statistically. We hardly know whether or not we benefit or harm our children — aside from the involvement of the religious element.

There are people here who are assimilated faster than the Norwegians. There are perhaps also those for whom the process goes more slowly. Some are engaged in ancestor worship; others are not. Statistics that would give us information about the second generation's relationship with the first would give us clear clues, when compared with our own estimates.

We have contributed abundantly of our resources to all possible causes; we have taken an interest in every activity we could except in getting an insight into our own social position. It is surely about time an attempt is made to clarify our situation.

Our people came to this country poor and with empty hands. In the course of half a century, they have acquired enormous areas of land and have transformed them from wilderness to rich and smiling landscapes, which will continue to be the homes for millions of human beings for hundreds of coming years. This is one of the greatest developments that has happened in history — this transformation of the prairie to fields, the opening of the greatest pantry in the world since the beginning of time. The Norwegians have exerted a great effort among the earliest pioneers. The least we could do would certainly be to see to it that their names would not be forgotten. And here much has already been lost. Of the over two hundred settlements whose history deserves to be gathered and preserved, only a dozen have been at least partially dealt with. Meanwhile, the old settlers die and so very important first-hand information is lost. It seems that we Norwegian Americans ought to be willing to give a small offering for the preservation of the names of our forefathers, who often lost their health and their lives in order to clear and smooth the way to prosperity for their families. As I have said, much has been neglected and there is much to catch up with.

It is probably superfluous to call attention to what a source of strength it is for a people to have a past — to know one's own family and to feel related to it. In our times, the owners of homesteads constantly change, and the son often does not seem to have the slightest reverence for the place where his cradle stood, or for the ground which his father cleared under conditions of great privation and hardship. There is no doubt of the fact that knowing the family history of such settlements will create a greater attachment for the home place. One of the greatest curses of success, prosperity, and culture is the growth of wanderlust which separates close relatives from one another and creates for all time a rootless family that does not have peace wherever it may be, nor does it attach itself anywhere.

The Norwegian Society decided at its annual meeting in St. Paul this year to get started on a statistical investigation dealing with the Norwegian-American people. It is also planned to get together as much historical data as possible about settlements and persons.

But in order to do this, funds are necessary. Even if they are paid promptly, the $1.00 dues which the members provide will not be sufficient for more than paying the necessary running expenses of the Society and of its quarterly publication. Research in statistics and history demands discerning and patient work and will need a man who can occupy himself exclusively with it for a time. It cannot be done without financial support.

There is not a Norwegian community, a Norwegian congregation, a Norwegian society, or even a Norwegian home that will not be benefited, directly or indirectly, by finding out what we are and where we stand. At least that is what we believe.

We have contributed thousands and thousands of dollars to colleges, hospitals, charitable institutions, and merciful purposes, in this country, in Norway, and in pagan countries. All this is good, and no one has become poorer by it.

The Society needs neither ten thousand dollars nor even a thousand. At most, there is talk about a few hundred, in order, as far as possible, to make entirely clear our own position here in this country, to prepare us for greater progress, and to make possible a larger vision in our endeavors in the future.

It is on this basis that we, on behalf of the Society, pass the hat around. Every donation will be acknowledged in the Society's quarterly publication. Exact accounts will be furnished the donors. Donations may be sent to the treasurer of the Society, Waldemar Ager, Eau Claire, Wisconsin.

VI

The Language Is Most Important

by Waldemar Ager

TRANSLATED BY LEIF E. HANSEN

EVERYONE seems to be in happy agreement that we ought to preserve our ancestral heritage as it is available to us in the form of religious beliefs, Norwegian literature, music and history, Norwegian sports, and the like. The fact that love for and interest in the roots from which we sprang is of great importance to us as character-shaping elements is no longer doubtful to anyone who has considered the matter seriously.

With this in mind, we have established a number of strong organizations among us — Norwegian churches, schools, social institutions, societies, and newspapers. A great number of these establishments — yes, almost all — have been built up with great sacrifice. None of them can be judged as having been disappointments. The demands have gradually grown greater, and we can safely say that little or nothing that

NOTE. Published under the title "Det vigtigste," this essay appeared in *Kvartalskrift*, 4–12, January, 1908.

is superfluous has been done in this area. We have taken pleasure in this work and have seen good fruits from it. But despite this fact, we can with absolute certainty say that all of these achievements — the visible products of our work — will be lost if the Norwegian language is lost among us.

There have been many who believed that the interest in things Norwegian would continue and grow even if use of the language disappeared. Many of our best people regarded the struggle to preserve Norwegian as a hindrance to our progress — something which has set us back and wasted time and energy here in an English-speaking country. After all, a language is only a collection of words of indefinite size. But experience has proved that with the decline of the Norwegian language there also falls interest for the rest of the ancestral heritage.

If there is an area in which the language ought to play the least role, then it would have to be in the church. But the late Gjermund Hoyme, president of the United Norwegian Lutheran Church in America, told me the year before he died that, in most places, attempts to use English in church services had been a disappointment. "The hymns and everything may be as correctly and as nicely translated as they could be, but it somehow doesn't meet the needs anyway," he said. In our town [Eau Claire], the young people demanded to have English services now and then — and got them. But those who so strongly urged this change were young people who themselves were good at Norwegian, but who hoped in this way to reach others of their age, who apparently did not have any interest in Norwegian or could not even understand it. However, the English services did not attract the youth to church, and so these services were eventually abandoned. There are places where an unusually talented minister who uses the English language can build up a large Lutheran congregation. Pastor Gustav Stearns in Milwaukee is an example. But all of those who know this able and gracious minister will say that he would gather a large crowd about him in a large city no matter which synod he associated with. And even in his congregation, there are now nine different nationalities represented. That will always be inevitable in such congregations. There is no accusation against them implied in this statement. It is natural that their development will take this course, and one must abandon any special promotion of the national heritage in such congregations.

The Lutheran faith is, in a special degree, one which a child is brought up in and not converted to. The veneration which attaches to the Lutheran name itself will be incomprehensible to people brought up outside this church. As a part of a child's religious training, there are implanted attitudes toward his parents, grandparents, and the many earlier generations which have sought their strength and comfort in life and death in this faith. One will perhaps not cut off these connections by using the new language, but psychologically there will be the effect of seeming to cut them off — and then most people will become indifferent to any such influences.

Experiments have shown how difficult it is to preserve the interest of youth in the faith and culture of its parents when the ancestral mother tongue is no longer used.

The German Lutherans published in English a splendid and well-edited paper for Lutheran youth. It was called the *Illustrated Home Journal*, and was modern in style and fully in keeping with the times. It had an enormous distribution among the several million Americanized Germans in this country and among other Lutheran youth. But it had to be discontinued. German-language Lutheran youth papers do well in a more limited field. For ourselves, we have an example, printed in Norwegian, in *Ungdommens Ven* (The Friend of Youth). This publication has grown and is a genuine success despite the contention that "young people want English." *Northland Weekly*, managed by the same capable man who edits *Ungdommens Ven*, and always equally well equipped, had to call it quits. The young people, who do not care about the language of their parents, do not appear to care much about their faith and history either.

These Lutheran youth publications have entered a field with considerable risks; for, as is well known, everyone talks about the necessity of keeping young people in the Lutheran Church, and yet we hear them for the most part speaking English.

There have been experiences, however, which have turned upside down many beliefs that once upon a time appeared to us to be incontrovertibly correct.

When Professor N. C. Frederiksen arrived in this country some twenty-five or thirty years ago, he believed, too, that the time had come to exchange Dano-Norwegian for English. In the latter language, he started publication of a very ambitiously planned periodical named *Scandinavia*. It failed with a great financial loss.

Some years later, a weekly in English for Norwegians was started in Minneapolis. This was *The North*. Heading this undertaking were some of the best and most talented Norwegian Americans in this city. We may never have had so well edited a weekly in the Norwegian language. Nevertheless, it also failed while, relatively speaking, papers printed in the Norwegian language gained an unbelievable circulation. An English-language periodical for Scandinavians, later published in Minneapolis, also was forced to cease publication.

A Norwegian periodical, *Vor Tid* (Our Time), in the course of two years achieved a very respectable subscriber list of 7,000 not including single-copy sales. However, the paper was finally discontinued, mainly because of poor business practices and not because there was no demand for it.

In my opinion, the efforts which have been made prove that if the language falls into disuse, then the interest for things Norwegian also dies. If we want to preserve and promote the interest for *norskdom*, then we must preserve and promote interest for the language. If that is lost, then, as it were, all ties are cut at once. I myself have to confess that I have yet to meet a single person of Norwegian descent who cared anything about the ancestral heritage and ancestral culture unless that person also understood the Norwegian language.

It is a near certainty that if we do not have the strength to awaken interest in the mother tongue and thus to insure a place for it among us, then the main achievements for which we have struggled will collapse.

We can gather together the history of the immigrants, but it will remain on the shelf unread. We can build churches and educational institutions, but eventually they will lose their characteristic value and slip into other hands. Our newspapers will disappear and the many magnificent organizations which have been founded among us will go out of existence. We can erect monuments, but they will lose their essential significance. We have had a series of important men who have spent their lives among us in the promotion of Christianity and culture. There will be no one to safeguard their memory, and much of what they planted will be trampled under foot.

It has provoked disgust among all civilized nations that the German government prohibits its Danish and Polish citizens from using their own language at public meetings. This is an attack on the sacred inviolability of the mother tongue, it is said. But one would think that the mother tongue would be as sacred and inviolable to us as it is to the Danes and the Poles living in Germany. If it is malicious to stifle love of the mother tongue among others, it must be worse to stifle it among one's own. History can establish, I believe, that no nation permits its language to fall into decay without penalty. Such occurrences are always connected with periods of decay in the life of a nation. If, on the other hand, giving up the language were absolutely necessary, then we would have to consider the die cast and allow ourselves to be absorbed in the mass of a new society. But no such necessity exists for us. It has been demonstrated here in America that immigrants have been fully as good citizens as the natives — and even better. There have been attempts to split the Union. One of these was made by the New England states — peopled by the descendants of the Puritans themselves. The second attempt was made by the aristocratic Southern states. In neither case were the so-called "foreigners" found fighting for the destruction of the constitutional government. The only attacks on the government of the United States have come from the purest native Americans.

As proof that we can preserve our own language and simultaneously be fully loyal and patriotic American citizens, we can point confidently to the best names that we have among us.

Immigration from Norway is not the result of political considerations. It has been an *economic* immigration. The Norwegians settled here in order to find better opportunities for a livelihood. They have had to seek these opportunities in a battle against nature and the elements and in competition with other national groups. What we have gained for ourselves has been honestly earned. Our settlers who cleared land here in the West often struggled under more difficult conditions than the Puritans had; the first colonists lived by the ocean and the rivers — and always had easy access to their home lands. The New England settlers have no greater historical claim on the Atlantic states than the Germans and Scandinavians do to the states in the Midwest. Why, then, should we display our subservience in such an exaggerated, humble, and prostrate worship of the Yankees? What *their* American forefathers have done for the country, ours have done as well. The accomplishment is not lessened simply because we still have a few of our own early pioneers among the living. And the Yankees do not ask for any special worship either. They are too "level-headed" for that. But there are a few among us who, in season and out, feel that they absolutely must assume a subservient position. They always find some situation which causes them to bow down.

Bjørnson wrote recently with respect to language coercion in Germany: "A nation need not go under, as long as it has two points of support — religion and the land. But if one deprives it of its mother tongue, in which religion is born and through which it is nourished, then one also deprives it of its religion."

Is this inescapable?

Yes, most will say. It is inescapable. We must prepare to switch over to English entirely. History teaches us . . .

To the contrary, history teaches us very little on this point. In America, there have been assimilations of races before — that is true of course. The Dutch in New Amsterdam, the Swedes in Delaware, the Germans in Pennsylvania, the French in Louisiana, and others. But one must remember that these occurred under different conditions. These people were far more torn loose from their own ancestry than we are from ours. For us the speedy means of communication, the newspapers, and the telegraph have, as it were, done away with distances. For example, one can get news from Kristiania (Oslo) in Minneapolis just as fast as one gets it in the towns of Norway. We can keep up with developments back home almost as easily as if we were there. There is considerable intercommunication. Thousands travel to their home lands each year and return with fresh impressions. He who wants to add to his enlightenment by keeping up with developments in his original country can do so with the greatest of ease.

Now we ascertain that we can maintain our own language as long as we ourselves wish to keep it. We can let our children learn it, if we consider that desirable. There is no inescapable judgment hanging over us in that decision. We can lose the language by letting it slip away from us voluntarily. No one *can* or *wants* to take it from us.

When someone states firmly that the Norwegian language *must* die among us here, at the same time he also says with equal assurance that there will come a time when we ourselves no longer will care about it.

But these prophecies sounded stronger twenty or thirty years ago than they do now. Thirty years ago everyone seemed to agree that the young Norwegians who grew up in this country would slip over entirely to the use of the English language. However, it is a rather peculiar fact that efforts carried on for the development of *norskdom* are made precisely by people who came to this country as children or who were born here. Those from whom we might expect the most — the newcomers — are most often keenest about Americanization. Often enough one may hear them speaking disparagingly about Norway, but such critical comments are very seldom heard from those who were born here.

In New York there is a Norwegian congregation which had a minister who was educated in Norway. The last year he was there, he instructed and confirmed all the children almost entirely in English. The congregation then called a minister who was born in Wisconsin, who had never been in Norway. When he came to this same congregation, he prepared all the children for confirmation in Norwegian. In Eau Claire, we have a ski club. The entire board of directors save one are men born in this country. When anything is to be done in our community in honor of Norway, the American-born Norwegians are more enthusiastic than the immigrants. Keeping in mind such phenomena, it is not altogether correct to say that the *youth* are ready to abandon the mother tongue.

Most of us will not be assimilated with native Americans, even if we ourselves would like to become assimilated in every way. We will not "melt into" Americans but into a mixture of Germans, Irish, Canadians, and the like. These national groups make up the population in the United States, where most of us live. We will *not* become "Americans" in any better sense than we now are. We will only lose our own racial characteristics without acquiring theirs. Everyone — including all races now in America — is, to a considerable extent, in the process of being absorbed in the melting pot.

The Norwegian Americans can be said to have entered upon a fortunate path for their own good, as well as for that of this country. These immigrants produce fewer criminals than the Americans. They are, on the average, just as prosperous. As pioneers, they have shown themselves to be as competent as the other Americans, and they are just as loyal citizens. They have already supplied the nation with evidences of significant mental abilities. In short, they have measured up — and then some.

There is a line of conduct which we ought to follow. We should attempt to continue on the same path and continue to "honor our father and our mother." In so doing, we shall prosper in the future.

But the most important, the life nerve of all of it, is that we must preserve among us our language — the language of our forefathers. Not as an inescapable evil but as a positive blessing. Cultured Americans teach their children French and German. Cultured people's children in Norway learn French and German, as well as English. Our immigrant children are not, I think, so poorly equipped by Our Lord that we should be unable to teach them Norwegian along with the language of this country. And, in addition, I would think that we are not so incompetent that we cannot get our children to comprehend that it is a sign of refinement to be able to speak, read, and write two languages.

We ought to make it fashionable to know Norwegian. Let young people understand that it is really a matter of being cultured to be able to speak both languages and to awaken their desire to speak pure and good Norwegian.

The Norwegian Society ought to regard as one of its most important tasks to work for the preservation and dissemination of the Norwegian language. An effective step would be for the Society to arrange declamatory contests similar to the well-known "Demorest Contests."[1] The Society could award a nice silver medal and a booklet of selected Norwegian declamation pieces. Youth organizations, lodges, temperance societies, and perhaps Sunday schools would then get a half dozen or more young people to participate in such competitions. The declamations would have to be chosen from selections made by the Society for this purpose. Instructions from the judges would be furnished. If a hundred such declamatory contests were held every year around the country, then the Norwegian language soon would be fashionable among the younger set, and that would perhaps also open their eyes to the literary treasures which the language has to offer.

This plan would not cost much to put into effect. The sale of booklets would almost pay for the medals. At the annual meetings of the Society or at major festivals, one could have ten silver-medal winners compete for a gold medal.[2]

---

[1] William Jennings Demorest was a New York reformer who worked for temperance and for the legislative prohibition of the sale of alcohol. In May, 1886, he launched a contest in which he distributed silver, gold, and diamond medals to the winners among young people around the world. These medals were won in elocution contests based on the best use of temperance tracts sent out from the National Prohibition Bureau, organized by Demorest in 1885. The contests became very popular and thousands of medals were won.

[2] The Norwegian Society eventually established declamatory contests of the kind

A suggestion has been made to make a memorial gift.[3] Many plans have been advanced, but none appears to have won general approval. I do not expect that the following one will, either. If all other attempts fail, however, perhaps we could also give this one consideration. We could erect a monument in honor of Norway in this country by gathering together a fund, the interest from which would be used for the promotion of Norwegian-American art, literature, history, and culture generally.

We do not need to set our sights so terribly high. Let us, for example, suppose that we could collect as much as would be required to build a single church or to pay a single teacher. Let us say that we could collect $20,000. Interest from this money, safely invested, would produce at least $800 per year for four prizes in the amount of $200 each, as an aid and encouragement to Norwegian-American literature, art, and historical writing. If we could reach no more than $10,000, well, then even prizes of $100 would be a great encouragement.

We will not honor Norway half as much by erecting ten statues, as by producing one single living individual of national importance. If we could only preserve the Norwegian language and our love for Norway, then Arctander's million lies in readiness here, when it is needed. And Kjetil Knutsson's school would perhaps come into being by itself and so also would the scholarship fund.[4]

I have — from the point of view of the Society — dared to write "The Language Is Most Important," as the heading of this essay. I do this because I fully and completely believe that if we permit the language to be lost, then anything else that we have in our hands will surely die.

---

described by Ager. These contests were given in memory of Sigvald Quale (1890–1909) with funds provided by his mother, Mrs. Anna Quale of Eau Claire, Wisconsin. The first declamatory contest was held in the South High School auditorium in Minneapolis on April 21, 1911, with about 1,500 people in attendance.

[3] The memorial gift refers to the plans to collect a large sum of money to present to Norway in 1914 when that country would celebrate the centennial of its independence. There were prolonged debates in the Norwegian-American press and elsewhere as to its use. In 1914 a fund was created from the money collected by Norwegians in America. The accrued interest was to be used for charitable and humane causes in Norway at the discretion of the Storting, the Norwegian legislative assembly.

[4] John W. Arctander (1849–1920) was a prominent Norwegian-American criminal lawyer in Minnesota. He was active in raising funds for public undertakings. The erection of a statue to the renowned Norwegian violinist Ole Bull in Loring Park, Minneapolis, was due largely to his efforts. As an appropriate memorial gift to Norway in 1914, Kjetil Knutsson worked for a national college at Eidsvoll, Norway, the site of the signing of the Norwegian Constitution in 1814.

VII

The Melting Pot

by Waldemar Ager

TRANSLATED BY ODD S. LOVOLL

ISRAEL ZANGWILL's drama *The Melting-Pot* became exceedingly popular among those individuals in our population who above all others consider themselves true Americans.[1] In their opinion, the theme of the book hit the target. These persons like to act as if they had opened a refuge for Europe's distressed, famished, and oppressed people. It is completely natural for them to assume that these immigrants must be utterly grateful for such an asylum, and that they consider it an obvious fact that the foreign-born must fuse with other immigrant strains and melt into something greater and better than they were before. Thus out of the melting pot will come a new person, a "Super Citizen," with all the best traits of the different races and none of the bad ones.

But the self-designated American himself does not wish to mingle with the foreigners. He doesn't wish to assimilate with them or to

NOTE. This essay, under the title "Smeltedigelen," was published in *Kvartalskrift*, 33–42, April, 1916.

[1] Israel Zangwill, *The Melting-Pot: Drama in Four Acts* (New York, 1909 and 1914, and a new revised edition in 1920). The play was first produced at the Columbia Theatre in Washington, D.C., on October 5, 1908.

absorb in himself the Russian, Pole, or Jew, but he wants these people to intermingle their traits with each other.

Theodore Roosevelt recently expressed high esteem for the German who would let his daughter marry a Russian. But Roosevelt himself would hardly permit one of his own daughters to marry any common Russian immigrant. The major intent and the general understanding of Americanization is simply that the immigrant is to be denationalized. The taking on of the character of the "new man" is of secondary importance. Discarding the "old man" is by far the more significant issue.

The play's title itself reveals a weakness. The melting pot makes one think of a melting together of metals. Here one is soon confronted by the fact that there are a large number of metals and that each has its specific advantage and usefulness. It would never occur to anyone to attempt to make a "super metal" — a product of all the best qualities in all the others — by casting them together. That would lead back to the Bronze Age. There is every possibility that the melting pot as an equalizer would destroy the best qualities in all metals and thus also end their useful values.

If one cannot as a matter of course cast all kinds of metals together without spoiling them, then one can perhaps even less likely melt together the different races without losing their strongest, most characteristic, useful, or attractive qualities. There are very few examples in history of beneficial mergers of races.

One can perhaps produce examples of a few racial mixtures, as for instance the Scotch-Irish, the Norwegian-Danish, or the Norwegian-Swedish. A successful mixture depends greatly on the circumstances under which the individuals have grown up, and there is no doubt that some racial mixtures can be desirable, especially when one race is decadent. But here in America it is a question of mixing together all possible nationalities, and this mixed race will grow up in a land which itself does not have any culture of its own and is, for that reason, unique. Now in this country, external conditions for a beneficial assimilation are extremely poor. Citizens of the new mixed society will grow up with the feeling that they are neither one thing nor the other.

As Dr. A. O. Fonkalsrud points out in his book *The Scandinavian-American*, the problem is made more difficult by the fact that it is completely impossible to determine any definition of what the genuine

American culture is.[2] One speech is valid in the New England states, another in the older Southern states, and on the West Coast one will be able to find something else again. There are no definite rules for what is truly "American." We encounter a culture which is regarded as being American, but on closer examination we find that it is "English" and that it has no more valid claim to be native here than the Norwegians' *norskdom* (Norwegianness) or the Germans' Germanness.

We Norwegians would for instance gladly melt ourselves into American culture, but we resist when we find out that it is not American but really English. We have the feeling that we can easily enough divest ourselves of the "old man" and strip ourselves of him, but the "new man" — the new dress — is made for others and by other measurements and does not fit us. We feel that it either does not cover our needs or that it lies in tight folds about us so that we cannot move freely. If we allow ourselves any self-criticism, we feel uncomfortable. Or if we act as if this dress does fit us, we make ourselves spiritual fools, because we don't permit ourselves any self-criticism. Well known is the type of Norwegian who is made fun of both by "Americans" and by his fellow Norwegian Americans for his burning and demonstrably idiotic attempts at acting like an American.

One can, I suppose, safely claim that the majority of Norwegian Americans in the cities have cast off their old dress without having been able to don the new one. Culturally speaking, they are naked.

They have book shelves but no books, except possibly the large decorative sets that are sold to the sort of people who buy in order to fill the inevitable bookcase in "Pa's den." Through conversation, one will find out that they do not read and have never read any kind of literature. Norwegian classics they cannot read, and an English or American book does not interest them. If they read anything at all, it is the most wretched and poorest fiction imaginable — the kind they find in some of the popular American periodicals. But as a rule, they only look at pictures, and it is extremely seldom that such an "assimilated" family knows the name of a single modern American writer.

They have expensive chairs without being able to sit comfortably in them and are actually often bothered by objects that originally were intended for comfort. They possibly adopt an English or American diet, but they have poor digestion and receive the most pleasure from

[2] Alfred O. Fonkalsrud, *The Scandinavian-American* (Minneapolis, 1915).

their table implements and the names of the dishes. From the uneasy and nervous position the housewife takes in a Morris chair to the sweating housefather when he, after the English manner, is forced to carve the roast at the head of the table, we get the impression that they are living in steady fear of revealing themselves. They seem to feel that the new garment — the "new man" — is a flimsy thing that slips away no matter how little they move. This kind of feeling is even found in our second and third generations. (It takes many generations to learn to cut the roast properly at the end of the table.)

In no field does the melting pot have greater possibility of success than in music. Here in some fashion, one can follow along, for the technical apparatus of music is the same for all peoples. In spite of the fact that there is a piano in almost every home and even on every well-situated farm — and the financial ability to have instruction is greater here than in any European country — we haven't been able to produce a single great musician. No musical training is considered complete without one's having been in Europe to learn some foreign national element or other in music.

In spite of all the pianos and all the financial ability, even the average interest for music is lower here than it is in the poorest European countries. One notices for instance how little singing there is by our young people. In the area of male singing, it is almost *only* the foreign-born that cultivate this art for itself. In the "American" churches, one hires professional singers to sing for pay — and very often they hire a foreign-born person to sing for them. The melting pot seems to cause a loss of the ability to enjoy music — and the musical ear disappears. Remaining is a more or less clear awareness that on many occasions music is necessary, and thank God it can be bought when it is needed.

There are hardly any immigrated races that do not lose some of their best qualities by coming into the melting pot. Perhaps more accurately they must have given up these qualities in order to become an acceptable mixed metal in the crucible. The Irishman seems to lose his sense of humor when he no longer feels Irish. The immigrated German is known for his integrity, stability, and responsibility. In Pennsylvania, where a great number of Germans have mingled in the general population, which one calls Pennsylvania Dutch, some of these qualities must have been lost. It is true that Pennsylvania has a reputation of being the most deprived state in the Union, and the phrase

"Philadelphia corrupt and contented" is sadly known. States where immigration is more recent and where assimilation is in its beginning — as in Wisconsin, Minnesota, Iowa, and the Dakotas — have been almost free from graft and scandals of the kind that have occurred in states where the melting process is more advanced. Also when we consider sobriety, Pennsylvania occupies a definitely unfortunate position. On the map of the Anti-Saloon League, it is the only completely black spot east of the Mississippi.

Concerning our own people, I will only point to one single characteristic that seems to disappear by assimilation: the ability to deny oneself less important objectives in order to achieve a more important one. The saga of our pioneers is one that everywhere speaks of self-denial. They could be content with little in order to save to buy their own home or to acquire a small basic fund for a modest business. This self-denial requires considerable character, if one is to pay off on a debt instead of spending money on entertainment, clothes, and the like.

The ability to deny oneself less necessary or superfluous things for basic needs is one that we can look for in vain in the majority of our "Americanized" youth. There are few Norwegian families in the cities that have not been affected by the fact that the children are completely different from the parents. They reveal a shyness for physical labor and in a way are stripped of the ability to save or to deny themselves — a tendency that ultimately drives the children away from home. The respect for the parents, passed down all the way from pagan times, seems to be lost in the melting pot. This trait they do not learn from the Anglo-American youth, who are very close to their homes. Our young people seem to lose their innate respect for father and mother without being able to acquire the Anglo-American love for the home. The melting pot does not produce good citizens, nor does it produce anything else that is good, unless one cherishes a definitely low and common standard as normal for everybody.

Mexico provides a rather typical picture of an assimilated population. It is difficult to determine what the so-called white population actually is. The stock from which they should have inherited most are the Spaniards, but one will look in vain for the proud Spanish love of country. Instead the Mexicans have retained the Spanish bull fights and the Spanish irresponsibility, cruelty, and lack of enterprise.

Our country does not need any more "Americans" in the sense in which we conceive the term. The mixed American is nearly the most useless citizen metal in the whole pot. As a farmer, he is far surpassed by the native Scandinavians and the Germans. It is persons of these nationalities who have created the dairy and cheese industry in the United States. They are the ones who are carpenters, lumberjacks, shoemakers, tailors, painters, and plumbers. They are the ones who build our homes and furnish them.

Other Europeans work in our iron and coal mines, our steel works, and machine factories — Poles, Bohemians, Italians, and others. It is Slavonians, Lithuanians, and Russians who work in the large slaughterhouses and carry forward the gigantic meat-packing industry.

When these people have entered into the melting pot, they no longer want to work with saw and hammer. They will no longer work in mines and steel mills or factories or slaughterhouses: they want to become insurance agents, politicians, and commission salesmen. Their children will no longer learn to perform any physical labor; they would rather starve or enter upon a career of crime.

If one doubts these conclusions, then one can stop and reflect on how few of the "assimilated" he finds in occupations that require heavy physical work.

One can perhaps observe these tendencies even more clearly among the women. The legions of prostitutes in this country are not drawn from the ranks of the poor newcomer girls, notwithstanding the fact that in certain quarters poverty is inaccurately cited as the major cause of prostitution. These women are most frequently recruited from the immigrants' daughters, who grow up with the feeling that they are something better and greater than their "old-country-ish" and hard-working parents. They have often not learned any mother tongue. The language they first learned was that of the street. Because of the language, they have not been able to learn to know their parents; their characters were not shaped in the home but outside of it. They acquired early the impression that they were superior to their parents, and the parents seemed to like the idea — it tickled their vanity or their foolishness. These daughters learned to look down on father and mother, and there could not be much pride in family and background to sustain them. In such homes, religious training is also usually worthless. Religious concepts often found expression only in the mother tongue, and family devotions conducted by the parents were often in the language that the children had come to consider obsolete and a mark of baseness and poverty. It is under such conditions that girls grow up with weak characters. They want nice clothes and amusements and consider physical labor below their station.

In Wisconsin, it appears that it is almost exclusively children of the foreign-born who fill the correctional institutions for delinquent youth. Of 349 boys placed in the State Industrial School in 1913–1914, more than 300 had been born in this country of foreign-born parents. Of 325 in the years 1911–1912, only 34 had been born of American-born parents.

There is much to suggest that those who have not entered into the melting pot are just those who engage in the heaviest work. They are more vital to this country than those who have gone through the process and have "Americanized" themselves and thus have surely become denationalized.

To this, one may object: Is it anything to strive for to perform hard and productive work? This question is best answered by recalling that it is those who perform this work and do it successfully who bear the nation's burden. They are the marrow and the core of the nation. This is not just a trite phrase.

We are surrounded on all sides by swindling, graft, and cheating. What else can one expect when in the cities only every fourth or fifth person works. Grown youths loaf around in schools for years because they are not inclined to work; in families with three or four grown healthy women, one must hire maids to cook the food and keep the house clean. Even in the lower middle class and in the working class, one can find that in a family of five or six grown individuals often only one or two are employed. As a rule, they are the two oldest, who from a physical point of view — or perhaps by advanced age — are the least qualified for it.

All this idleness and the "want-to-be-elegance" constantly tend to create the possibility of existence by sponging off the productive groups. Is this anything to aspire to as a race?

But there are even worse consequences of the melting pot. An always valid evidence of a nation's strength and viability is its reproductive ability — the ability to propagate. Without children being born into the world and the race continuing to grow, nine-tenths of what a nation achieves is meaningless.

There are no available statistics, but all my personal experience indicates that in our assimilated population of Norwegian descent in the cities, there are sadly few children. It is, as it were, in the air that it is "unrefined" to have children — in any case more than two. The "Americans" have, as everyone knows, seldom any more. One of the first things a young newly married woman finds out when she associates with "the swells" is how to avoid having children and even how to induce abortion. For a woman who has been brought up on the deeply despised "old-country-ish" principles, it is a sin to kill the unborn child. One will regard each child as a gift from God, which it surely is. According to one prevailing notion in certain city circles, a child is a nuisance, a plot against the freedom of the mother, a burden on the family. A condition which in one language is often designated as "blessed" is characterized in another as "trouble." There is nothing that is more quickly learned in the melting pot than that children are a result of carelessness, revealing little sense and consideration. Having many children is plebeian, common. To this may be added the well-known rule that when there are only one or two children in a family, they will usually be spoiled. The assumption that one can bring up two children exactly five times as easily and well as ten holds water only if one considers their upbringing only as a question of money and education. Otherwise one will find that children are better behaved, stronger, and less spoiled in large families than in small ones.

We must never lose sight of the fact that the term melting pot does not involve the real Anglo-Americans, who have retained the language and culture of their homeland. What we have had of cultural life has just about completely confined itself to the so-called New-England-Americans, and even to a limited area where they have been able to develop with the least amount of outside influence. One recalls at random names like Longfellow, Bryant, Poe, Emerson, Whitman, Holmes, Hawthorne, and Stephen Foster. Since the golden age of such men, something has obviously been lost in the melting pot even when it concerns the New-England-Americans. But we are indebted to their two hyphens for this flourishing period in the cultural life of our country, otherwise so culturally poor.

We recall the two major types from England — the English Commoner and the English Cavalier. These types we find during the great crises our country has had to endure. From the Revolutionary period, we have Benjamin Franklin and George Washington, from the Civil War Abraham Lincoln and Robert E. Lee. Zachary Taylor and Winfield Scott are a third pair, Webster and Calhoun a fourth. No nation has produced stronger or more noble characters than these. If the "Anglo-Americans" enter the melting pot, then our country will never again produce men of this type.

America also has a racially mixed type. We recall men like Roosevelt and La Follette. Viewed in light of what we have said above, one will quite soon — in spite of the many good and excellent qualities of these two men — notice something unfinished in them. There is not the genuineness, the completeness, that characterizes the pure and refined English types. Their great energy is explosive, uncontrolled, and reminds one too much of a display of fireworks.

If you encounter the genuine New-England-Americans, you will find a type so far different from our Norwegian "want-to-be-Yankees" that you could cry at the comparison or laugh yourself sick — as you perceive the different aspects of the foolishness of their imitation. From an "American" point of view, the melting pot is thus not for "Americans." It is its function to denationalize those who are not of English descent.

If this process succeeds, then one can imagine a servile, weak, and imitative lower class, which has lost the strongest and most forceful traits of its character and which subordinates itself to the only pure race. This latter race will become a kind of automatic upper class.

The worst possibility, however, is that the people of non-British descent who are made over in this manner may come to form a dead weight in the nation instead of constituting its major source of energy, as they now do.

There has been considerable talk about the supposition that the immigrants, through the very process of melting together, would be able to give the nation their best qualities. Against this argument stands the indisputable fact that they are, or will be, robbed of these qualities before they voluntarily enter the melting pot. Take for instance the pride in family and race, which is one of the basic elements in a strong character, in religious culture, and in much else. The first condition one notices when Norwegian Lutherans organize an English-Lutheran congregation is that it ceases to be a church for the people, a church for ordinary workers with equality for everyone accepted as a matter of course. In such congregations, lesser importance is attached to religious instruction, and outward embellishments become more conspicuous.

The two major qualities of a good citizen are character and a sense of duty. The Norwegian who was a good citizen in Norway and became just as good a citizen in this country will also become a good and useful citizen in Canada if he settles there. He will be — and ought to be — welcome wherever he settles. He carries his good citizenship with him because it is based in his whole character and upbringing. His love of country can be a declamatory topic. Love for justice and respect for the law and success in his work are of immensely greater value than love for the country and the flag, because this kind of patriotism has not shown itself steady in any country. In America, we had of course the great Civil War, which proved how little the love of a certain number of square miles is worth when one's own interests or one's own corner of the country are thought to be in danger of being molested.

First and most importantly, one owes it to one's country to stand guard over one's own character — and to go into one's work with all one's strength without letting anything of value be sacrificed.

VIII

The Melting Pot Again

by A. H. Lindelie

TRANSLATED BY ODD S. LOVOLL

Among the things which I took along on my journey in the way of reading material was the last issue of *Kvartalskrift* published by the Norwegian Society of America and edited by Waldemar Ager. As I think highly of and admire Mr. Ager, I read *Kvartalskrift* first. The lead essay has the title "The Melting Pot."

The article in question is a critique of Israel Zangwill's play *The Melting-Pot*. This drama has likely been read by only a few of *Normanden's* readers, but quite a few have probably seen it as made into a moving picture. The main features of the plot are a portrayal of personal persecution and oppression in Europe, especially in Russia, and

NOTE. These comments on Waldemar Ager's essay in the April issue of the magazine were printed under the title "Smeltedigelen igjen" in *Kvartalskrift*, 108–113, October, 1916. As an introduction to Lindelie's article here, Editor Ager wrote in the same issue of *Kvartalskrift:* "In *Normanden* (The Norseman), Mr. A. H. Lindelie has objected to my article entitled 'The Melting Pot' in our April issue, and, as he is also a member of the Society, we are printing here abstracts of two letters which he has written during his journey to the east and south." Lindelie's first letter to *Normanden* was dated in Chicago on September 13, 1916. His second letter, written from New York, was also reprinted from *Normanden*, dated September 17, 1916. *Normanden* was a successful Norwegian-language newspaper published in Grand Forks and Fargo, North Dakota, from 1887 to 1954. A. H. Lindelie had served as managing editor of this paper from 1895 to 1898.

of how the emigrants find shelter in the United States and become a part of this nation.

This drama, which has gained great popularity over the whole country, is, however, a thorn in Mr. Ager's flesh. He maintains that Americans do not at all wish to become assimilated and that Americanization only means that the immigrants are to be "demoralized" and cease to be Europeans. Just as the melting together of different kinds of metals will not produce a new metal, Mr. Ager is of the opinion that different nationalities cannot be melted together without destroying them. Later he asserts that "there are no definite forms for what is 'American.'" But what is considered to be "American," Mr. Ager finds to be "English," which "has no more valid claim to being native than the Norwegians' *norskdom* (Norwegianness) or the Germans' Germanness."

"We Norwegians would for instance gladly be assimilated into 'American' culture, but resist when we find out that it is not American but English," Mr. Ager continues. He believes that those Norwegians who make an effort to cast off the Norwegian culture and don the "American" make fools of themselves, and he declares that "culturally speaking, they are naked."

Mr. Ager states that the Norwegian "Americans" have book shelves without books, except for the decorative sets, which are intended to fill the shelves and not to be read, and that they read nothing except possibly the wretched popular American periodicals. They have expensive chairs, but are not able to sit in them, and this "applies even to our second and third generations," he says. He adds that they have pianos in abundance, but that they cannot play them; they have even lost their ability to enjoy music.

Where the immigrants are so recent that they have not suffered from melting together, as happens in the West, he claims that they are superior in both political and moral respects.

After having treated everyone alike, Mr. Ager extols our pioneers for their industry, thrift, and love for the home, but he finds that the children are a bunch of "good-for-nothing" individuals, who through their Americanization have lost their parents' culture. He says: "They do not want to engage in physical labor; they want to become insurance agents, politicians, and commission salesmen." He asserts that this applies to boys and girls and to "the legions of prostitutes in this country . . . [who] are most frequently recruited from the immigrants' daughters." Pride in family and race disappears with Americanization.

The idea Mr. Ager advances is then that people of every nationality which immigrates to America should live separately, speak their different languages, develop the culture they brought along, not intermarry, and most importantly not become Americanized. He believes this last because Americanism is the same as Anglicism, for which he has an aversion that is touching.

Although the article is written in Mr. Ager's usual captivating language, I cannot help registering a protest and asserting that Mr. Ager must have been in an exceptionally bad mood when he wrote about "The Melting Pot." On the other hand, he was in a cheerful mood when he wrote another article, a review of Dr. Evjen's latest book.[1] This volume tells about individuals from Norway who came to this country in 1630 and later. It appears that quite a few Norwegians settled in New York and in other places in the New England states in that period.

In this article, Ager relates with zest that these persons and their descendants married into Dutch and English families and became progenitors of the Vanderbilts and families like the Bayards, DeLancys, De Peysters, Van Cortlands, and Van Rensselaers. Mr. Ager asserts here: "It means much to us that we participated all the way from the beginning and constituted a part of the embryo out of which the United States grew."

This conclusion is surely true in all respects, but one puts the magazine down with the question: How could one and the same man write both articles?

One would have expected a denunciation of these emigrated Norwegians of the seventeenth century because they were so depraved that they went into the melting pot and because they married godless people of other nations, forgot their language, became culturally naked, and were the ancestors of families that belong to New York's "400." They were depraved also because their descendants were dipped in and smeared with Anglicism, until they now belong to the class which today is among the carriers of the despised "American" culture, which according to Ager, is only English.

[1] John O. Evjen, *Scandinavian Immigrants in New York, 1630–1674* (Minneapolis, Minnesota, 1916). Dr. Evjen was a professor of church history at Augsburg Seminary in Minneapolis.

In his first article, Mr. Ager begins with the assumption that the immigrants to this country bring with them a culture. Now, I will not maintain that the immigrants from Europe are cannibals, because, of course, that they are not. But on the other hand, they are not all cultured people either, who bring with them literature and musical instruments. It must be admitted that the great majority come here "naked" in regard to culture; so they have nothing to cast off when they arrive. They have hardly heard the word "literature" and have never seen a piano. When the second generation procures book shelves and pianos, it is of course progress that must not be made fun of, even if the books are not the best that exist, and even if they can play only "My Country, 'Tis of Thee" on the piano.

In other words, Mr. Ager's starting point is a mistaken assumption. There are only few — extremely few — who come here dressed in the garments of culture.

But the metaphor itself, which Mr. Ager employs, is unfortunate. A person cannot simply "cast off" or "put on" culture. Culture penetrates deeper; it goes all the way into the blood, and it is not possible to change the blood. And genuine culture is sympathetic understanding. It treasures everything novel, understands what is new, and can easily assimilate it without losing anything of its original content. The quality which Mr. Ager complains is lost is only a veneer; it lies only on the outside, and it rubs off and an English coating is put on instead. Thus it represents no great loss.

Even though the Norwegians are among the best immigrants which America receives, does Mr. Ager maintain that they all — or even most of them — are cultured people? If this is so, can he then explain what has become of their culture and cultural needs upon their arrival — actually before they have learned a single word of English? They do not bring along a literature, and they buy no books here. These facts Mr. Ager and other Norwegian-American writers know well from their own experience. The immigrants do not even read newspapers. They do not know what music is. They are, in other words, devoid of intellectual interests. There are, of course, exceptions, but they really are exceptions, and not, as Mr. Ager has made it appear, the rule.

At the same time that I do not rank the pioneers' cultural position as high as Mr. Ager does, I do place the second and third generation much higher than he does.

The early immigrants became farmers and laborers; the sons go to the dogs, he thinks. In this Mr. Ager is greatly wrong. There are a great many immigrant sons who are farmers. Out in the West, we see them coming by the thousands from Illinois, Iowa, Wisconsin, and southern Minnesota to settle on homestead land or on farms they have bought. But not all of them become farmers. The rest become merchants, lawyers, doctors, and bankers in both the old and new settlements. Not a few become teachers, ministers, professors, and the like. In cases in which the father was a railroad laborer, the son may become a conductor. Where the father was a carpenter, the son may be a foreman, or established in his own business. There are fewer of the second generation than of the first who drink themselves to death. I find progress and not decline.

The immigrant daughters receive a bad testimonial from Mr. Ager. Again he has confused a small minority with the majority. It is of course not denied that some walk the ways of vice or become useless, but Mr. Ager ought to know that this is a small group. Most immigrant daughters become mothers, after having worked for a while as teachers, stenographers, store clerks, or in other useful occupations.

Can it be Mr. Ager's opinion that the immigrants' children should be nothing more than their parents were? There are only a few immigrants who at their arrival are qualified to be merchants, bankers, doctors, and lawyers. Why should not their descendants occupy these positions rather than turn them over to the "Americans"?

Whether or not there is something which can be called Americanism, I will not comment on at this time. My protest against the Norwegian Society of America for abusing the immigrants' children will have to suffice here. I am myself a member of the Society, but Mr. Ager's article I cannot accept.

It was not my intention to mention my friend Mr. Ager's name in this letter [the second to *Normanden*], but I cannot restrain myself, and I will explain why.

In New York there is a company which has large automobiles to take passengers around town and show them its attractions. The town is divided into three parts: the residential area in the upper part, the business district in the lower part, and the Bowery and Chinatown at night. These tours I advise everyone to take. Each tour costs only one dollar, and a guide describes all attractions.

A. H. Lindelie

I have just returned from the lower part of town, and now Mr. Ager will catch it.

Our guide routed the tour through the foreign section on the East Side, and for a whole hour we drove through the Chinese, Greek, Polish, Italian, Jewish, Dutch, German, Hungarian, and other districts. It was on a Sunday afternoon, and so we saw people in their Sunday best. Every nationality is represented in numbers from 20,000 to 100,000 people who live segregated from the others. Here are separate cities within a city. Here are foreign nations within a nation.

In this area, the melting pot has not been able to begin its mission. Here we find every nationality with its own language, traditions, and customs, "culture," religion, and the like. Here no one has "cast off" his culture, and no one is "naked," as Mr. Ager would say. In these places, there ought to exist the ideal of which he is so passionately fond; here there is no Anglo-American culture to poison the air. Here every nationality is "itself and enough unto itself, so damnably complete."[2]

It will require eight pages of *Normanden* to relate what I saw; therefore, a few exclamatory excerpts will have to suffice. God deliver and save us from an America of that kind! Bring out the melting pot! The result cannot be worse than what we have now! Bring out the American culture, whether it is English or something else! Throw the whole thing into the casting ladle!

When we drifted away from Mr. Ager's ideal and into the Anglo-American culture, oh, what a relief! As Norwegian as I am, there was still something in it that I felt akin to. What happiness among the "de-nationalized" people, and what misery among the "cultured" Europeans, who have not cast off their "culture."

In my first letter, I forgot to refute an important point in Mr. Ager's article on the melting pot. He maintained that the State of Pennsylvania is hopelessly corrupt and habitually drunken because the immigrated Europeans were "de-nationalized" and have become Anglo-American in culture.

Mr. Ager is wrong. Make a journey through Pennsylvania's iron, coal, and industrial districts and see the cities in these regions. The immigrants are not melted together, they live segregated, they form nations within the nation, and they constitute the mass of ignorant voters, which the saloon element uses to keep corruption going. They more than offset the good, Americanized part of the population.

[2] A paraphrased quotation from the play *Peer Gynt* by Henrik Ibsen.

The metaphor of the melting pot is not meant, as Mr. Ager makes it out, to indicate that different kinds of metals are to be melted together. The words mean that scrap iron, rusted iron, unused iron, and good iron ore are to be melted together in order to manufacture steel — good American steel. It is people who are to be melted together and not people and cattle and fish and wild animals.

IX

To Mr. A. H. Lindelie

by Waldemar Ager

TRANSLATED BY ODD S. LOVOLL

IN YOUR discussion of my article "The Melting Pot" in the Norwegian Society's *Kvartalskrift*, you make objections that I consider it my duty to respond to.

My article was not a critique of Zangwill's play *The Melting-Pot*. It was a treatment of the general question of the melting pot, and the title was used because the above-mentioned drama has gained acceptance as a description of the process of assimilation which is occurring in this country.

I have not in any way passed judgment on the "Norwegian" American; I am myself a Norwegian American. My parents lie buried in American soil, my children were born here, and I do not know of any other home than the one I myself have struggled to build in this country. But I mentioned different features I have observed in "Americanized" Norwegians. I have in mind those who try to pass themselves off as completely American and have destroyed all bridges behind them. Such people do not want any association with their coun-

NOTE. Using the title "Til hr. A. H. Lindelie," the editor responded to Lindelie's comments on "The Melting Pot" in the same October, 1916, issue on pages 113–119.

trymen; with them assimilation is to be considered an accomplished fact. They are individuals who, in other words, have come so far that they have fulfilled the requirements made by the melting pot and have lost, or behave as if they have lost, their identity as being of *Norwegian* descent.

The real American has retained his identity as being of *English* descent. The nation's language, its institutions, its manner of public debate, its judicial system, its literature, and the like all bear witness to this fact. And concerning it, there is, to my way of thinking, nothing to comment upon except to say that we also ought to retain *our* identity as a race to the degree that it is possible. I believe that we should also try to make our contribution, as the English have made theirs, to build up this country.

There is nothing disloyal in this. There is hardly a biography of an outstanding American written without looking back many generations to establish his descent. The best American families we have are aware of their ancestry and are proud of it. They have strong family traditions. They have not attempted, and do not attempt, to pass themselves off as something which they are not. When it concerns melting together with other nations, they are in no way eager. That is one of the reasons why members of their churches are mainly of the upper class. Those who have sought to enter into better American social circles will perhaps have made the discovery that it is neither accomplishments nor money which opens or closes the doors, but much more their descent and family connections.

I have not said that our daughters go astray and tread on the paths of vice or become useless and that our sons become bad. What I emphasized was that such a characteristic as "family pride" plays an important part in keeping young people away from the ways of evil. I believe this to be as certain as anything can be. If the feeling of kinship with one's own family stock is lost, then one has less with which to resist wickedness, and there must, I suppose, be some reason for the disproportionate increase in the percentage of criminal acts in the second and third generations. Here statistics speak. I have concerned myself all the time with the young people who grow up under circumstances in which they have been taught to look down on their parents and their family heritage as something poor and objectionable. I have not used the expression "demoralized" but instead "denationalized."

Let me inform you, Mr. Lindelie, that I am so good an American citizen that I feel I owe my country my best effort to contribute. If my experience indicates that Norwegians in America decrease their ability to contribute by breaking down all bridges between themselves and their past, if they lose features in their character which make them strong and traditions which make them faithful, then I contend that it is to the detriment of the country, and I consider myself entitled, even obliged, to say what I mean.

What I wrote is only expressed as personal observations — the total impression I have received of the process of assimilation. Others may use different standards of value and arrive at completely different conclusions. And when I used expressions which treated everyone alike, then it was because I, of course, knew that there were exceptions and that it is a sum total that is meant and not the individual numbers.

As far as the Norwegians who immigrated to New York in the seventeenth century are concerned, they did not become Americanized, for the reason that no "America" existed. The Dutch were Dutch, the English English. Our countrymen assimilated with the Dutch and the Dutch eventually with the English in the century that followed, and then I suppose they melted with the "Americans" again in the next century.

The most valuable contribution was made in the beginning, when they participated in shaping the embryo out of which the nation sprang. The races which were later absorbed — the Dutch, the French, the Swedes, and the like — were not much in evidence when the nation was "born." The English were the only race that had retained its language and racial stamp, and this race it was that carried the national development forward. So *English* were they in every respect at the beginning of the Revolution that they had no thought at all of a break with England.

Foreign names that appear alongside of Washington's — like Lafayette, Steuben, Pulaski — were clearly foreign in this country. These men could hardly speak English. The "Super Citizen" of the melting pot did not participate in any conspicuous degree in American life.

You have a different conception from mine of the culture brought in by the immigrants. You mean nice clothes, good manners, and accomplishments of different kinds.

Let me now remind you of something. Many of the poor newcomers, even those who arrived before the Civil War, had perhaps only had an "ambulatory school" education. Their clothes were simple, they lived in dugouts or in miserable log cabins, they did not understand the language of the country. Still they assembled and discussed American politics and were vitally interested in the slavery question, the tariff, and other current issues. They might trudge for miles over rough paths to hear a political address or to attend a church service. They not only built churches, but they also frequented them. We find that they might even enter into intense controversies over theological questions. And all this while they were still relatively young people.

How much of this breadth of interest do we find in our "Americanized" countrymen? In our Americanized youth? Even in our high-school educated young people?

I was sitting in the pulp mill of a sawmill in Norway on one of the last days of June, 1914. It was during the noon break. The workers were discussing the royal murders in Sarajevo and the possibilities for a world war. It was the first time that I realized that there was a serious threat to world peace. Such concern for public affairs I call culture.

In the fall of 1915, I was present in a family gathering in which the housewife mentioned that the high prices were supposedly caused by the war. A grown girl, pretty as a picture, equipped with the formal education that is given here, opened her lovely and surprised eyes and directed the following question to her mother — and it burned itself deeply into my soul: "Is the war yet?" The world war had then lasted more than a year, and so it had not completely slipped by her that there was a war.

As far as appearance, formal education, and manners are concerned, this girl would be placed infinitely above the previously mentioned sawmill workers, if one uses such factors as a standard of measurement.

I see that the young newcomers from Norway gather nowadays in Good Templar lodges, found singing societies, present plays, and do much more. Nevertheless, these young people came out of the labor class in Norway. There is no doubt that they possess something that the majority of our American youth lack. It is extremely seldom that the latter begin anything or apply themselves to any cultural cause. Whatever is done for the youth in our own town is always done by older people. It is they and not the youth who lead.

Why is it so strange that I with such experiences arrive at the conclusion that our ability to contribute is decreased as assimilation goes forward? And it occurs to me that whatever we can retain of our most valuable characteristics will benefit the country.

Let me give just one example to illustrate what I mean. It is natural for Norwegians to be in opposition, to give their opinion, even if they possibly personally will make enemies. The Americans let things go carelessly rather than risk personal confrontations. How often it happens in legislatures, city council meetings, school board meetings, and the like that so-called "genuine" Americans have shoved a Norwegian forward and said: "You say it! You bring the matter before the house and we will back you." In both the Minnesota and the Wisconsin legislatures, we have examples of such men being pushed to the front with a reform program at an early stage when it cost something to take a position. I imagine that an assimilated Norwegian in such cases would expect one who was not assimilated in the same degree as he himself is to be the one to express truths, which another man believed in but which that man did not dare to speak for in public.

Mr. Lindelie has visited New York's foreign quarters and seen Chinese, Jews, Poles, Italians with all their peculiar ways and he exclaims: "God deliver and save me!" From what shall He save you, Mr. Lindelie? Be honest now — don't you mean that God will deliver and save you from such kinds of citizens? But how are these poor people to be "assimilated"? Mr. Lindelie, you do not want to associate with them, the ones that you ask God to save you from. You do not want to absorb these people into yourself either, these strangers from whom you also ask God to save you. But if they are to be assimilated, they must fuse with us who are already acclimated —, spiritually speaking. But you do not want to. We do not in all truth want to either. Who are they then to be melted together with in a great unity? Oh, they can mate and melt together among themselves. Let, for instance, the Jew take the Italian woman and the Pole the Greek woman. "Into the melting pot with them all!" exlaims Mr. Lindelie.

But you yourself then, Mr. Lindelie, genuine Norwegian that you are, are just as Norwegian as the Jew in New York is Jewish and the Pole Polish. Now what shall we do with you? The casting ladle is also waiting for you and into this ladle you must enter together with all these people that you pray God to deliver and save you from. You hesitate — it was not this way you meant it. That might well be, but that is the way it is. We cannot arrive at a homogeneous population until the northern races are mixed with the southern ones. You have to enter the pot. If you consider yourself too good, too superior, then you are a poor American citizen according to your own prescription. It is just people like you who are needed in order for the melting to be successful and for the new citizen metal to acquire the pureness and brilliance which you certainly missed in these, our fellow wanderers, whom you observed.

I have an idea that when our parents came from Norway — or perhaps when we ourselves disembarked in New York or when the first settlements were in the making — then there was many a Lindelie who turned up his nose and prayed God to deliver and save him. But see what kind of fellows these Lindelies have become. This has happened despite the fact that we Norwegians in America have retained our Norwegian language and our Norwegian names, and read Norwegian literature, and belong to Norwegian congregations and societies, and give speeches in Norwegian and write in Norwegian papers. We have even become such good citizens that we can ask God to deliver us from other immigrants, who have come after us. Are not these good results without calling upon the miracle of the melting pot?

You wish to inform us that it is the large foreign element in Pennsylvania that has given the state its poor reputation. You have noticed the industrial cities with their foreign character. But now the true situation is that Pennsylvania earned its poor reputation before this relatively recent population was able to assert itself. When Lincoln Steffens wrote his articles about Philadelphia's being "corrupt and contented," that city was listed as the metropolis, which of all the country's large cities had the lowest percentage of foreign-born citizens.[1] Since this "God-deliver-and-save-us-element" has gained some influence, Pennsylvania has made great progress in decency and is in the process of recovering from its bad reputation.

All large cities in any country usually have sections where one must ask God's protection. This situation mainly has its cause in the poverty and vice associated with such cities. But how is one to judge? It is possible that Mr. Lindelie on Wall Street and Fifth Avenue would have

[1] Lincoln Steffens, "Philadelphia Corrupt and Contented," in *McClure's Magazine*, July, 1903. Reprinted in Lincoln Steffens, *The Shame of the Cities*, 193–229 (New York, 1948).

found nicely dressed people who were bigger crooks and much more dangerous to the welfare of the nation than these poor "God-deliver-us-people" in New York's foreign quarters.

There are many kinds of people in Norway with divergent dialects and ways of life. When temperament is concerned, there is as much difference between people from west and east Norway as there is between Scots and people from Valdres, folk who live in eastern and central Norway. But there has never been discussion of any melting pot in Norway. One is of the opinion that all these individuals are needed, and that their differences enrich the country. These people are all good Norwegians. There is a marked difference between residents of Copenhagen and of Jutland, but in Denmark there is no agitation for any melting pot. And Denmark is as compact a state as one can find anywhere and is even a model for enterprise, co-operation, and general education. Germany at present gives such an example of co-operation, energy, and public spirit — in proportion to population — as the world has never seen before. This country is made up of such widely different kinds of people as Bavarians, Prussians, and so forth. No nation in the world, however, can demand more of its citizens.

Still — let me tell you: These people who, you think, live their own lives in New York do have a folk life to exhibit. For painters, writers, sculptors, and musicians, there will be infinitely more inspiration to draw upon in the poorer areas than on Fifth Avenue and in Central Park. Have you noticed our new literature from Upton Sinclair's *The Jungle* to Zangwill's *The Melting-Pot*?[2] These writers seek inspiration from the districts in which a folk life is being lived and in which really genuine personalities exist.

[2] Upton Sinclair, *The Jungle* (New York, 1906).

X

The Great Leveling

by Waldemar Ager

TRANSLATED BY LIV DAHL

As might be expected, the so-called anti-hyphenism campaign has lately gained new support. On the surface, everything seems convincing: one language, one culture, a uniform mode of thinking, no foreign gods. A complete leveling of anything of non-British or non-Anglo-Saxon origin, values, however, which to some extent still preoccupy the minds and hearts of the citizens.

Everyone knows that great diversity exists between the peoples of various nations. As a result, Europe has become rich and multifaceted. It would be difficult to imagine France — or Paris — without the French language, the French tone, and the indescribable feeling of being in another world as soon as you cross the English Channel. We cannot imagine Holland without the Dutch and their particular ways, Germany without Germanness, the Mediterranean countries without their diverse populations and distinctive ways, or the Eastern countries without their Eastern culture. Even based on external clues, we un-

NOTE. This article has the title "Den store udjævning" as published in *Kvartalskrift*, 73–89, July, 1917. It was the first of a series of essays under this heading.

derstand the abundance that is represented in the cultural variety of these people.

No American would like to see this diversity leveled out. Nobody enjoys this "Europeanness" more than the Americans.

Suppose it would be possible to erase these differences. Italy without the peculiarities which now characterize its population, the Orient indistinguishable from the Occident, nothing to make the Bedouin or the Arab different from our black Americans. Women everywhere wearing the same costumes, thinking similar thoughts in the same language. No burnoose for the Arab, no blouse for the French, no coat for the Tyrolean, no caftan for the Jew. Everybody dressed in Adler's Collegian Clothes, or Styleplus, or Kuppenheimer's "made in U.S."

No minarets, no Greek cupolas, no gondolas on the Canale Grande, only ferry boats of standard type. No Cathedral of Cologne or Notre Dame nor a Cathedral of Trondheim — Billy Sunday tabernacles instead, practical, appropriate places of worship — where souls may be saved 66 per cent cheaper than in any other religious structures.[1] Everything molded in a uniform Anglo-American form. How poor this would make Europe! Not because the substitutions in themselves were less valuable, but because of the lack of diversity.

Culturally, the leveling could be compared to the killing of the creativity of whole nations. For a long time, we have realized that the magnificent Italian music is born out of the Italian folk life, not through correspondence courses in harmonics and composition. We got Hungarian music from the common life of Hungary, and German music from German folk traditions. When Jenny Lind and Christine Nilsson went out and conquered the world with their song, it was particularly with folk ballads springing out of Swedish peasant cottages. In the valleys of Norway, one found music unequaled in other countries, and masters like Ole Bull and Edvard Grieg scored international triumphs with characteristic manifestations of the Norwegian folk soul — a soul which was created by a peculiar and distinctive ethnic life and nurtured under peculiar circumstances. And the entire world became richer.[2]

This folk personality may be found in the architecture of a country,

[1] William Ashley Sunday (1862–1935), called Billy Sunday, was an American evangelist.
[2] Jenny Lind (1820–1887) and Christine Nilsson (1843–1921) were celebrated Swedish operatic and concert singers. Ole Bull (1810–1880) was a popular Norwegian violinist, and Edvard Grieg (1843–1907) was an internationally famous Norwegian composer.

in its literature and in its pictorial art, as well as in its music. It is this wealth which culture has drawn upon throughout the ages. It is as important for nations as it is for individuals to have a distinctive character.

We may even take a step further and say that it is imperative to have a soul of one's own, that is, for oneself first, but also for the sake of others.

It is possible for individuals as well as for entire nations to manage without or with a partial soul — one which is not one's own. If one succeeds in convincing some individual or nation that it is preferable to be without a soul, then it is rather easy to provide that individual with a bit of it for household use. It is always convenient to have some.

People who accept a sort of adopted soul are both quick to learn and obliging. Quick to learn because they never raise objections, and obliging because an instinct of self-preservation tells them that the bit of soul given to them is dependent on the master-servant relationship. They can always put two and two together, and they are afraid that they may be destitute as far as their inner selves are concerned.

In Norway you may still meet farmers of the old school, who talk about the cotters of earlier days, how all their thoughts were concentrated on the welfare of the farm, without even expressing as much as a wish to see the farmer's parlor. This was before they started subscribing to newspapers and taking part in politics, before they had giddy thoughts about owning property, or providing their children with knowledge beyond that which was strictly necessary.

Such was the case with most of the Negroes during the time of slavery. The memoir literature of the South is full of examples of their praiseworthy loyalty, through which they helped their masters prolong their own bondage. History also indicates what happened when "Massa" no longer provided them with soul.

An individual without this inner life may become an excellent worker. He calls his master's horses *his* horses, the fields his fields, and the farm his farm. The master's politics are his, and the master's happiness, his happiness, and when the master coughs, *he* hawks also.

From the viewpoint of the master, such a worker is worth his weight in gold, much to be praised and in every way desirable. He does not strike, he does not ask for higher wages, he does not count the hours. Altogether, he is excellently suited for the master's needs.

Older Norwegians — or those who were cotters in Norway — will remember the expression of true pain, indignation, or surprise on the master's face when he, self-consciously twiddling his cap between his hands, confessed that he was considering immigrating to America. Others had the same experience when they subscribed to newspapers and told their masters that they would try to get a piece of land for themselves. Or when their children wanted to learn something, or perhaps when they started singing a song they had written, or when they surprised those around with ideas they themselves had originated.

In such circumstances, the master was deeply disturbed. The beast apparently had a soul. This thought created great uneasiness. What would he need a soul for? The farm was not his and could never be his. How was this to end? He did not mind that Lars smoked cigars, as long as *he* had given them to him. He did not forbid him to wear a top hat, as long as he himself had worn it first. But Lars, infected by the corruption of time, went ahead and selected his own hat, even put it on in a tilted manner. This could never end well. The farmer did not mind having Lars on the town council, as long as he was there on behalf of his master.

Workers without any personalities of their own were in many ways fine — servile and loyal. The most inviolable loyalty could be read from their grateful and adoring dog eyes. How easily they forgot brutality, how thankful they were for each kind word. They were unrivaled in thanking their master for everything.

But servants never discovered anything. They were not able to improve on anything. They were as poor when they left the farm as they had been when they came. They left no trace, except for the tracks from their wooden shoes. These shoes they always left outside the door when they went into the master's kitchen to eat, because the wooden shoes were noisy, and there was something almost religiously quiet and proper about being in stocking feet when they went in for a meal.

The time did come, however, when the master realized that it was better to allow the cotter to keep his soul unimpaired. This was useful in many ways. He gained initiative, he became more self-sufficient, and the farm was better off because of it. His understanding and insight resulted in money in the bank for the master. New land was cleared, improved work methods were introduced. The master gained respect for other people's souls now that he saw that they could be useful to him. The cotter was welcome to a mind of his own as long as possessing it brought prosperity to the farm.

The Americans of British ancestry did not give up their inner lives. They broke away from the political system of the British empire; they did not give a hang about the king and the prerogatives of the Crown. They set up their own political housekeeping and were prepared to defend it with their blood; but they did preserve their language, their traditions, their ethnic temper. They needed that to live like human beings — nothing else would do for them. Such a heritage cannot be purchased or manufactured. It must be passed on from generation to generation and be preserved or it will be lost.

No Americans were more patriotic than the New England poets of the first half of the last century. But their poetry was patterned after the British model. They sought inspiration in English patterns, found nourishment which suited their cultural life and built on that. But it was not American — not what was eventually to be accepted. In the South — in Virginia, the Carolinas, and Georgia — lived people who were patriotic to American ideals, but, to the extent that they could afford it, they settled like landed gentry, and acted like the English aristocracy to which they felt they belonged. They kept their soul — they bled for it with remarkable persistence during the 1860s. But there were others who lost their English cultural heritage. They were looked down upon — even the slaves looked down on them. They were "the poor white trash."

They were English like the others, but they had lost their heritage. With it they also lost their initiative, their ambition and zest for work. In this rich country of America, a class of utterly destitute, ignorant whites sprang up. They did not want to send their children to school and did so only when strict laws compelled them to. Anyone who has traveled in the South with his eyes open has been impressed by its poverty and lack of enterprise.

A man associated with our town's program of poor relief assures me that the most utterly destitute people he deals with are descendants of families who have lived here for generations. Even in the country, you find them living in poor circumstances to a much larger extent than do the immigrants.

And yet, a class of half-wild white people sprang up in this country. Read the history of Kansas, or the accounts of Bret Harte and of other

American authors from the early mining towns and gold-digger camps of the West.³ The lynchings are perhaps the most easily perceptible proof of the lawlessness common at this period.

Milwaukee is perhaps the big city regarded as being the most foreign. However, to the praise of Milwaukee it should be mentioned that — in spite of its breweries and saloons — it ranks lowest among the large cities in its crime rate. The population, largely German, has preserved a great deal of respect for law, order, and discipline, a part of the spiritual luggage they brought with them across the ocean.

In the cultural domain as elsewhere, the rule applies that he who has much shall be given even more; but it is also true that he who has little shall lose everything. The more one has of one's own culture, the more easily one may acquire the culture of others. Nobody better appreciated the greatness of Germany than the Scotsman Carlyle; the best history of English literature was written by the Frenchman Taine. Danish literary critics were the first to understand the great Norwegian poets, and to the enormous quantity of literature on Shakespeare, the Dane Brandes contributed more than anyone else.⁴

Let us look at some more immediate examples. The well-known Professor Julius E. Olson in Madison was born in this country. *His* two great men — those whom he puts above anyone else — are Henrik Wergeland and Abraham Lincoln.⁵ I have never met a Norwegian more enthusiastic over Wergeland or an American idolizing Lincoln more than Olson does. These two personalities are very different; they have only one quality in common, kindness of heart. Olson devoted great attention to one of them, and therefore he could also express considerable devotion to the other. His ability to appreciate Lincoln and to be moved by him was that much greater because he had also been affected by another great personality. Because he understood one, he also understood the other. He gained insight thereby, and no doubt his ability to influence others increased because he had received inspiration from such different sources.

Or consider Rasmus B. Anderson.⁶ His immense ability to work,

---

³ Bret Harte (Francis Brett Harte, 1836–1902) was an American writer.

⁴ Thomas Carlyle (1795–1881), Scottish historian, philosopher, and essayist. Hippolyte Adolphe Taine (1828–1893), French critic and historian. Georg Morris Brandes (1842–1927), Danish literary critic.

⁵ Julius E. Olson (1858–1944) was professor of Scandinavian in the University of Wisconsin at Madison from 1884 to 1935.

⁶ Rasmus B. Anderson (1846–1936), Norwegian-American scholar, editor, and dip-

his persistence, and his willingness to tackle the most thankless and tiring tasks are typically Norwegian. Think of all his excellent translations — the great quantities of Norwegian and historical literature which reached American cultural life through him. As you do this, you realize how important Anderson's enthusiasm for everything Norwegian was to the American people. Minus this Norwegian fervor, he would have disappeared into the masses, perhaps with narrowmindedness as his most notable attribute.

Again, consider Knute Nelson. How utterly impossible to think of him as a leader like Joe Cannon or a dozen others.[7] It was Nelson's particular Norwegian characteristics which our country needed in the national legislative assembly. He had that trustworthy, solid, granitelike personality, with the traits which several Norwegian rural politicians had: the ability to get to the core of things, to the axis around which the total chaos was spinning. There was no lack of orators in this country, but there was a scarcity of those special qualities possessed by Knute Nelson. Remove these, and what is left? The country was enriched because he had a Norwegian source to draw from.

In our state of Wisconsin, there are more people than in Norway. More people live in cities where they have easier access to education. The state is very scenic. We have lakes and fishing, and our forests are famous. Memories of Indians, settlers, hunting, and trapping are still quite fresh. We once had extensive lumber traffic and the colorful life that accompanied it. And there was the Civil War with its deprivation and suffering. All this — or at least some of it — ought to have left traces in the state's literature. There were possibilities for creating something typically American, something of our own.

But we got nothing. Hardly a name to warrant even a modest place in a literary history. And in this state lived, and still live, descendants of such literary and book-loving people as the Scandinavians and the Germans. No painter, musician, or sculptor of any note has appeared. Not a single, solitary accomplishment in the arts.

The sad fact about a cultural heritage is that when it is lost, it is impossible to retrieve it either through purchase or as a gift. With it, as

---

lomat. He was professor of Scandinavian in the University of Wisconsin from 1869 to 1883.

[7] Knute Nelson (1842–1923) was a Norwegian-American politician. He served as United States Senator for Minnesota from 1895 until his death in 1923. Joseph Gurney Cannon (1836–1926), American lawyer and politician.

with sight, when it is gone, it is gone forever. Nobody can fill empty sockets with sighted eyes. But, more than anything else, a cultural heritage consists of the ability to "see things."

Literature may be cultivated by filling up book shelves with sets of books, which are never read. We have lost the ability to be deeply influenced by a good book, a beautiful poem, a lovely tune. We do not "see" anything particular in it. This carries over to other areas, too. We have difficulty feeling moved by anything outside our own private circumstances and our own financial interests. To be taken in by a book salesman is no sign of culture.

A painting becomes simply a picture, with the frame the essential feature; it is that which attracts the eye. Music — piano music, for example — disintegrates into cling-clang, ping-pang sounds which follow each other, fast or slow, in certain rhythms. In the concert hall, if the pianist impresses us, we applaud until the artist returns to the stage. We feel that we have done a good deed, even if we have to suffer through another piece of music.

It has been my lot to deal with a number of young people who were born in this country to Norwegian parents: splendid youth whom I have encountered in organized temperance work, in lodges, and youth organizations during the last thirty years. Among these, I remember only one or two young people who had read books and had known about their authors. One of them had spent several years in Norway. Many, many of them had never read anything except school books. And this in cities with large free libraries. These youth were not prevented from reading because of lack of time either.

In our town the only ones with literary interests are old ladies. The town's Women's Club features a subgroup which engages in reading and "study" of literature.

Our land is rich in many ways, yet it is not rich when it comes to literature and art. However, the Anglo-American cultivated his heritage until he could create something of his own. And if there is good soil and it is cultivated, something will at last start to grow. Nobody can predict what that will be; it arrives as a force of nature, but in stony ground nothing will grow.

The New England poets constituted the English cultural aristocracy in America. They had difficulties approving anything which did not measure up to English standards. Those who went their own way often ended up as drunkards and forlorn individuals. That is what happened to Edgar Allan Poe and Stephen Foster.[8] But to their credit, it can be said that they were faithful to their English heritage, even though they were a part of American life. Yet it was not their lot to produce anything typically American. That contribution came from quite unexpected quarters in the guise of American humor.

We did not expect the development of such humor at all. The puritanical surliness and the most holy soberness — which even the politicians worked into their carefully composed phrases and which appeared as verbal antics — were relieved by a liberating wit. This was a kind of humor which differed from any other because of its assumed seriousness. Puritanism had given birth to a bastard, one who poked fun at its own father. Never had anyone seen such a child before; but the child went out and conquered the world.

He came quite naturally and unexpectedly — such children always do — and was healthy and lively as such children almost always are. The cultural aristocracy of New England did not acknowledge his contribution. Nobody owns to such children. They were scandalized by him, as we always are by such children.

American humor sprang out of the West, and it did not originate with people who had studied literature. Most of the first humorists had learned their language at the type cases of small newspaper printshops. Petroleum V. Nasby, Josh Billings, Artemus Ward, Bill Nye, Bret Harte, Mark Twain — as far as I can remember, they were all typesetters at one time in their lives. Few things amuse such artisans more than typographical errors or wrong spellings. Nasby, Billings, Ward, and Nye were masters of ludicrous language with apparently serious intent. Not even the atrocities of the Civil War could keep people from smiling at their wit. The famous Nast sketched the most celebrated American political cartoons, which can truly be said to surpass those of any other country.[9]

But this breakthrough of American humor would not have been

---

[8] Edgar Allan Poe (1809–1849), American poet and short story writer. Stephen Collins Foster (1826–1864), American song writer.

[9] Petroleum Nasby, pseudonym of David Ross Locke (1833–1888), American humorist. Josh Billings, pseudonym of Henry Wheeler Shaw (1818–1885), American humorist. Artemus Ward, pseudonym of Charles Farrar Browne (1834–1867), American humorous writer. Edgar Wilson Nye, called Bill Nye (1850–1896), American humorist. Mark Twain, pseudonym of Samuel Langhorne Clemens (1835–1910), American novelist and humorist. Thomas Nast (1840–1902), American caricaturist and illustrator born in Germany.

possible if the New Englanders had not maintained their English heritage. These people read a great deal and enjoyed what they read. Good soil existed.

To what extent are we indebted to this phenomenon of humor in the country's literary history? The American brand of wit was moral. It was not dirty like some of the French and Scandinavian humor. It is not replete with stories of excrement and the like which mar much of the Norwegian humor. There is rarely any levity about poverty, old age, or sacred things. Profane language seldom exists; yet this literature has been considered funnier than that of any other country. Had it not been so extremely difficult to translate it, it would have cleansed the world from the type which in itself is so dirty and sordid that nobody can call it true humor.

All these creators of American humorous literature were of Anglo-Saxon origin. Immigrants of other nationalities did not contribute to it.

Many books were written in this country, but it took time to find a literary form which was our own. Not even General Charles King with his fifty-six novels from the Civil War can claim to have created a new literary form.[10] But when the discovery of gold in California attracted a certain type of people, a distinctive and remarkable culture evolved. It turned out that a new form — a typically American literary form — could be created. This was the American "short story." It differs from short stories of other countries in that it has a plot and an independent structure. It is a novel in condensed form. When we have read one of the better examples, we are left with the impression of having read a great novel. We know the characters in depth. Take for example Bret Harte's "The Luck of Roaring Camp." It may be read in less than half an hour; but we remember everything, and it is forever imprinted in our minds.

The most celebrated author to visit this country in the last century was the English novelist Charles Dickens. He was great and inimitable. We would never have originated the American short story had it not been for our reverence for Dickens. His influence is easy to trace, and the creators of the American short story are Anglo-Saxon Americans. We of other immigrant peoples have produced no one to match these writers.

In places where an original culture is created, there will always be

---

[10] Charles King (1844–1933) wrote about army life in the Civil War and on the plains.

possibilities for a distinctive literature to develop. When Alaska attracted gold diggers and fortune seekers, a unique culture developed under remarkable conditions. Examples of worthy literature were created. This happens inevitably and naturally when there is good soil. Nothing special is required in the way of interesting characters. In Jack London's best novel, *The Call of the Wild*, the hero is a dog. In the stockyards of Chicago where a large number of Lithuanians work, a special culture has sprung up. Upton Sinclair's *The Jungle* pretends to be a product of socialistic agitation, but it is truly American literature. So is *The Pit* by Frank Norris.[11]

But those who have given us what we have of typical American literature are Americans of English descent. This came about because they were the only ones to preserve their heritage.

When the American ambassador Walter Hines Page recently gave his great speech in Plymouth, England, he said, among other things, about his fellow citizens in this country:

"They have not only outgrown in numbers all the British elsewhere, but they have kept what may be called the faith of the race. They have kept the racial and national characteristics. They have kept British law, British freedom, British Parliaments, British character, and they are reared on English literature. I am not boasting of my own land. I am only reciting how your race had endured and survived separation from you and your land. Our foundations were British, our political structure is British with variations; more important still, our standards of character and of honor and of duty are your standards, and life and freedom have the same meaning to us that they have to you."

Hardly anyone in this country would raise his voice in protest against such a statement. Nor would anybody accuse the Anglo-Americans of being less patriotic Americans even if they cared for their heritage to such an extent that a man in high political office could say this on behalf of the nation.

We Norwegians are happy that the Americans have retained their relationship with England. We owe them great gratitude for having preserved this heritage, for having kept the characteristics of their origin, and the national traits so as to benefit the culture of this land.

But we cannot render *our* contribution on the basis of their heritage. If we are to contribute anything, it must be on the basis of our

---

[11] Jack London, *The Call of the Wild* (New York, 1903). Frank Norris, *The Pit: A Story of Chicago* (New York, 1903).

Norwegian heritage. We do not say that it is greater, for that it is not; nor do we say that it is better. But we must say that it is ours, and we must make our cultural contribution on the basis of it, if we are to offer anything at all of value to make the country richer. It is what we *have* and the Anglo-Americans *do not* have which must be the basis for our contribution to the cultural household of the nation.

To illustrate, let us discuss our spiritual effort. Norwegians take the evangelical attitude more seriously than do Anglo-Americans. There is more inside and less outside. There is a considerable difference between a Norwegian Methodist congregation and a typically American one. Doctrine and discipline are the same; the worshipers sing the same hymns and observe the same rituals. There is no tendency among Norwegian congregations to make their churches institutions of entertainment, as is often the case among the Americans.

Perhaps even greater differences may be observed between Norwegian and American Congregational churches. The Norwegian Congregational churches are, as far as I know, distinctively evangelical. Greatest emphasis is placed on a personal life in Christ, and the service is characterized by that approach. The great American Congregational churches are principally engaged in religious philosophy instead of in the direct preaching of God's word. The "spirit" is entirely different, although the preachers are educated according to the same principles. There is no disagreement in doctrine; the discrepancy arises in the interpretation.

It would benefit both the American Methodist Church and the American Congregational Church to adopt part of the Norwegian interpretation. They would benefit from it and perhaps be the first ones to desire it. But this contribution cannot be made by the Norwegian Methodists and Congregationalists unless they themselves keep their diverging views. Should they become Americanized, then this important contribution will be lost. If a sour dough is to work, it has to have the characteristics of a sour dough. Should it be sterilized before the flour is mixed in, it will be less than useful.

The Norwegian Lutheran urban congregations are typical "folk churches"; the American Protestant urban churches are rarely so. According to the minister of one of the three largest American congregations in our town, you can hardly find as many as half a dozen working-class families in his church fellowship. He grieved at that. In the Norwegian Lutheran congregations here, 90 per cent are workers. As a rule, the American Lutheran congregations are not folk churches. How useful it would be to preserve this Norwegian trait of Lutheranism. No great and universal American Protestant folk church exists. The common people — those who are less well off — are snatched up by the Catholics; they have the greatest folk church.

Occasionally one hears American ministers — whose honesty, piety, and personal religious convictions are beyond doubt — joke in the most irreverent way about God and heaven, the devil and hell. They may do so, apparently, without anyone in their congregations taking offense. Norwegian-American ministers could not do that.

What I have stated here fits other situations as well. It applies even to practical pursuits. Comparatively speaking, Green County is the richest county in Wisconsin. The cheese manufacturers have produced this wealth. Years ago Wisconsin cheese was almost a blot on our state's reputation. It was known for its poor quality and distasteful odor. Then Swiss people moved into Green County and started making cheese according to old-country methods. This cheese found such an extensive market that all the other manufacturers adopted the practice of the Swiss. Laws were passed to protect the cheese against "American" influence. Today Wisconsin cheese is renowned for its fine quality, and it represents one of the most important sources of income for the state.

Norwegian fishermen on Lake Superior as well as in Alaska have had a similar influence. They take advantage of the riches of the lakes and the sea by treating the fish in a Norwegian manner. This way of doing things has benefited the entire country, and everyone has gained through the displacement of American methods.

What I intend to convey is that, in order to increase the wealth of the nation, we must contribute something of our own, something valuable and something which the country needs. And the country needs everything we are able to preserve from our heritage. But what we do not preserve, we cannot contribute to the culture here.

It has been said — and it is supposed to be true — that French women dress more tastefully and less expensively than any other women. This is a desirable trait which could be transferred to others. But when the French woman ceases to feel and behave in a French manner and has gone through the melting pot, then this characteristic will be lost. She does not at all distinguish herself from the women of other countries.

It has been said about us Norwegians that our best quality is our willingness to work. That has caused Norwegian laborers to be highly regarded in Wisconsin. But it is difficult to detect this attitude in the grandchildren of the settlers. Their industry is more often below than above the average. Statistics from the reformatory of the state, the Boys' Industrial School, provide figures that are anything but flattering to us.

Norway is a small nation. If any country needed uniformity as a girdle of strength, Norway would be the one. Yet, there is great diversity there in language, temper, and philosophy. People of Western Norway are as different from those of Eastern Norway as both groups are from people in Northern Norway. Each valley offers something unique in taste and in manner of living. Each sectional group possesses abilities and talents of its own. In Norway it is assumed that this variety makes the country rich; no one wishes at all to level everything. Neither is there any desire to create a new type of person by melting together people from the districts of Valdres, Nordland, and Østerdal in order to erase the differences. One strives rather to preserve them, and over and over again new cultural values from these sections are discovered. Every now and then some remote community surprises the nation with an additional contribution to the country's wealth, beauty, culture, or honor.

We have recognized the stimulating value that comes from traditions — this noblesse oblige, which does not apply to nobility alone. The women of Hardanger are known to be able seamstresses and good at crafts. This is a general characteristic. It would be shameful for a woman from Hardanger not to be dexterous. This skill has not only been useful to the people from that district; it has benefited Norway as a whole. It has created an industry, half art and half trade. The influence has reached far. I knew a Norwegian woman in Chicago some time ago who made a living from teaching Hardanger embroidery to Americans.

If the women of Hardanger had ceased considering themselves a part of their local heritage, and if everything that reminded us of Hardanger folk had been leveled, then, of course, their excellence in embroidery would have been lost along with other crafts which were rooted in tradition, as well as in popularly developed artistic sense and appreciation.

Of course, these people are *Norwegian*. Who would stand up and say that those who attempt to preserve the uniqueness of their community in Norway are not Norwegian? They are Norwegian to such extent that many people regard them as the only true Norwegians.

It is often the case that people of a foreign nationality settling in a new country can contribute to their adopted land just what it needs the most. The first voices in Norway to speak up for Norwegian independence were Danish. They *saw* what the Norwegians themselves did not *see*. Heroes such as Colonel Ulrich Kruse and Colonel Wilhelm Jürgensen were Danes.[12]

Norwegians have always exercised great influence in Denmark. Names such as Holberg, Steffens and Wessel are closely identified with the cultural independence of Denmark. They were better Danes than the Danes themselves, even if they were Norwegians and felt like Norwegians. They understood national conditions which the Danes were oblivious to. Rye, Schleppegrell and Helgesen were Norwegians. The Danes considered them their best army commanders in the war of the 1840s. They brought victory to Denmark, and two of them died for Denmark. It would be hard to find truer and braver Danes than these Norwegians.[13]

In Norway there are a great number of Danes who consider themselves Danish and are called Danish by the Norwegians. But now they are Norwegian citizens. One of them is at present the mayor of Kristiania (Oslo).

In these two countries, there is no demand for any casting ladle or melting pot. The process of fusion must progress naturally; that is the only way it can come about. If we are true to ourselves and do not try to be something we are not, then superfluous national characteristics will wear away little by little, and essential ones will take their place. The process will go on without loss.

This melting cannot come about by a sudden catastrophe or by decree. The Russians tried it in Finland and the Germans in Schleswig. The results do not invite imitation. The same thing can happen when an individual declares: "No more Norwegian for me" — or "From now on I shall divorce myself from everything that ties me to the Norwegian people."

We may *say* these words and perhaps *mean* them, but our resolve is

---

[12] Ulrich Christian Kruse (1666–1727), officer in the Norwegian-Danish military forces. Wilhelm Jürgensen (1762–1842), Norwegian military leader of Danish birth.

[13] Henrik Steffens (1773–1845), Norwegian-born Danish philosopher and natural scientist. Olaf Rye (1791–1849), Frederik Adolph Schleppegrell (1792–1850), and Hans Helgesen (1793–1858) were Norwegian-born military officers in Denmark.

doomed to failure. The man does not become an American; instead he becomes a monkey, a mimic who never in his life will be a true American.

We are Americans in the sense that we feel this to be our country, the flag our flag, and our interests identical with the interests of the nation. We are Americans to the extent that we wish to live in the country and for the country, and if need be, to die for it. This is the way we should be and must be, if we are to take our citizenship seriously. If fate leads us to Canada, we are obliged to live in the same way there. It is a question of honesty, loyalty, and sense of duty.

However, if we do not possess these qualities as Norwegian Americans, we certainly cannot acquire them by changing name and language and clothes and religion. We cannot get them by removing ourselves a thousand miles from the closest Norwegian — or by thumbing our noses at the country in which our own cradle or that of our parents stood.

XI

The Citizen and the State

by Waldemar Ager

TRANSLATED BY CARL H. CHRISLOCK

Ever since the day — and perhaps much earlier — when someone showed Jesus a coin of the realm and requested an explanation of the sensitive issues of the people's relationship to Caesar (the state), the following problem has been open for discussion: Where do my responsibilities to the state terminate? How much can it rightfully demand of me? Where is the boundary limiting what it can demand? On the one hand, there are persons who contend that we owe the state everything — our lives, our interests and cultural capacities, our material possessions, our children's lives, and our energy. In addition, since God established the state to rule over us, we owe it unconditional obedience in every area of life. On the other hand, we find those who argue that originally a governing body was merely a necessary evil and that its existence as a dominant force in our lives today lacks credible justification. Differing from this anarchistic viewpoint, but nevertheless a threat to the state's divine origin and to absolutism, is the concept

NOTE. This essay is Part III of "The Great Leveling" series. It was published under the title "Forholdet til staten," in *Kvartalskrift*, 37–50, in the April, July, October, 1919, issue.

holding sway in democratic countries today. This view denies an obligation to the state per se and holds that the state is rather the people's own creature and servant. The people exist not for the sake of the state, but the state exists for the sake of the people. This concept underlies universal suffrage, and the popular election of officials, legislators, and judges. So we have rule of the people, for the people, and by the people.

Christ's interpretation of these questions was simply that one should render to Caesar what is Caesar's and to God what is God's. For those present and listening, this reply was not entirely complete, but it had the virtue of being applicable to all states, all peoples, and all situations in every epoch. In allocating responsibilities in those days, one had to distinguish between external and internal obligation. There was a domain outside the jurisdiction of the ruling power. The state was not absolute — not even mighty Rome in relation to the oppressed and helpless Jewish people.

The reply of Jesus conveys an impression of being evasive, but its impact was that of a cleaving sword. The keenness of the weapon obscured the reality that its apparently mild blow would forever separate political power and the freedom of the spirit. Like the one delivered by Saladin's sharp scimitar, which beheaded the felon with such lightning speed that the body remained upright and the head momentarily in place, this blow also was seen as a flash. For centuries afterward, mankind failed to understand that Christ's words had shattered an ancient concept of the state as God's deputy on earth.[1]

A modern interpretation of the response of Jesus would read something like this: You shall discharge your duties to the state in areas that rightfully belong to it, but you shall not worship it, idolize it, or render to it that which belongs to God. You shall not assign any divine attributes to it. In other words, you shall adapt to the nation's laws and ordinances in your conduct and civic activity, but you shall not permit a political rule to mold your soul, your cultural life, your ideals. It is to almighty God and not to a temporal power that you owe an accounting of your spiritual stewardship.

But again the stubborn question emerges: What essentially belongs to the state's domain? What to God's? Where is the boundary between what is of the flesh and what is of the spirit?

[1] Saladin (1138–1193) was sultan of Egypt and Syria.

Here it must be said that even if one cannot precisely define the dividing line one can certainly interpret the great military invasions that have occurred as clear examples of moral transgression. Every Belgian knew that the Germans had overstepped the boundary when he received news of the storming of Liege, the occupation of Brussels, and the siege of Antwerp. To search for the exact line as evidence of the invasion would be ridiculous. How and where the state invaded the spiritual realm is also easily demonstrable.

In times past and to some extent today, mighty princes and nations have usurped what belongs to God in order to consolidate their power. On the other hand, ecclesiastical authorities (particularly in the Catholic Church) have sought to appropriate both what is due to God and what belongs to Caesar. We have had both clerical states and state churches, rulers of God who were holy and religious or holy prelates whose personal style of life and sphere of activity were exceedingly worldly. Ostensibly they represented both God and Caesar, or Caesar and God — a divine structure on a secular foundation or a secular structure on a divine foundation. From mankind's standpoint, these are the most unfortunate combinations that world history has recorded for the unprejudiced reader.

No state has wholly succeeded in separating secular and spiritual authority. Here again the concept of the state's divinity assumes the most diverse forms. We hear, for example, that authority is instituted by God — yes, *all* authority. This, however, we cannot understand. We are almost compelled to see the concept as a ghostly survival from the days when one of the state's functions was to protect God from human deceitfulness. This led, among other things, to the burning of Protestants in Catholic lands and of the so-called witches and sorcerers in Protestant countries. The day the temporal rulers first appeared as God's guardian and protector was a disastrous one for Christendom. And we are not completely liberated today. We do not deny that all authority is instituted by God, but neither do we wholly understand the concept. "Bathhouse John" and "Hinky Dink" of the Chicago City Council installed by God? Or Governor W. L. Harding or the wrestling promoter whom Harding invested with authority to prevent congregations in Iowa from worshiping God in languages other than English? Are people who win elections by means of corruption, bribery, and wire-pulling installed by God? Was the flock of grafters who built

Pennsylvania's state capitol holy and of God? Was the Czar of Russia holy? Or Kaiser Wilhelm of Germany? Or King Philip of Spain, one of the monarchs who most frequently emphasized his divine mandate, who laughed only once in his life — at the time that he received news of the St. Bartholomew's Day Massacre in Paris? Was he installed by God? Satan could not have done worse.[2]

The Bible does not convey the impression that the state is holy. The prophets were nearly always at war with it. Some of the prophets were monstrously disloyal — and that to a government which more than any other could claim to be holy. For a state to avoid setting itself up as an object of worship always has been difficult, particularly in turbulent times when much is at stake and the greatest sacrifices are required.

However, it is worth noting that a particular state never accepts the divine origin and mandate of other nations. Each believes only in its own. States beat each other down if they can and pray to God for help in so doing. At the recent Peace Conference in Paris, the delegates of only one power voted against punishing the former Kaiser Wilhelm; that was because they regarded his person as inviolable. This vote was cast by the delegates from non-Christian Japan. Italy, England, Belgium, and several other countries which have inviolable kings — and France with an inviolable president — did not believe in the inviolability of any head of state but their own.

Nor do the people themselves give much weight to the state's sanctity, infallibility, or unassailability. The American Revolution was economic in nature. The American patriots believed that King George was installed by God only until enactment of the Stamp Act imposed heavy, extraordinary financial burdens on the colonists. When the ruling power of Britain ran athwart the economic interests of the colonists, they raised the standard of revolt, and the holy state of yesterday became so unholy today that they had to break loose from it and create a new one. Sanctity was obliged to yield to economic interest. Recently one has seen ancient monarchical lands, in which the sanctity of authority was a dogma, drastically transform their governments without regard to divine origin and holiness. The notion of a direct identification between the human institutions and God apparently rests more on expediency than on reasoned belief.

[2] Governor W. L. Harding issued his "Language Proclamation" to the people of Iowa on May 23, 1918. It prohibited the use of foreign languages as a medium of instruction in schools of any kind, in public places, and in addresses.

When all is said and done, continuity is not characteristic of the state. Our American constitution is relatively new, but it is still one of the oldest in the world. How transitory ruling bodies are and how quickly they are restructured! They frequently mend and repair their fundamental laws. Last year's fidelity can become this year's treason, and what was lawful last year may be unlawful this year. The state is not an object of worship; it is a governing apparatus that should be directed by the people, an administrative system which constantly changes in response to the needs of the time and the interests of its citizens.

The state is not even equipped to superintend the people's morality, except insofar as it seeks to restrain immorality in areas where the security and health of citizens are threatened. In a democratic country, official ethics can never rise above the level on which the mass of the people stand. It is more likely to be lower than higher. The history of liquor legislation illustrates how public opinion forced the government to enact national prohibition against its will. The people's morality must be raised, it seems, if that of the state is to be elevated. A democratic country will always reflect the demands of popular majorities. If it fails to do this, or for its own security seeks to create a friendly public opinion, or employs coercion to impede opposition, it is becoming autocratic or is already so.

Autocratic rule claims dominion over conscience, and demands blind obedience. Under such a government Caesar demands what is God's. It says: You have only to obey. The state assumes responsibility before God.

American political theory assigns to its rulers only what is due Caesar, that is to say, the state shall be a completely secular governing apparatus. Thus we were given a free country that refrained from coercing the consciences of its inhabitants. This country recognized no church as belonging to the nation as a whole, and when it excluded religious instruction from the schools, it did so because this activity was perceived as lying outside the state's domain.

It is only recently and under the special situation created by the World War that our government has begun to emerge as guardian of the people's thought and conscience. We recall the official warnings issued at the beginning of the war in Europe cautioning Americans not to form any opinion with respect to it or to take sides, an extremely difficult if not impossible feat for thoughtful human beings.

Consider also Stephen Decatur's famous words which for a long time embellished the editorial pages of many newspapers and by official arrangement were projected on the screens of moving picture theaters: "My Country! May it ever be right — but right or wrong — my Country!"[3] Clearly this statement means that patriotic considerations demanded a readiness to do wrong when the state — one's own state — advocated it. To do wrong is sin. A citizen had to be prepared to do evil when the interests of his country required it. Thus it is right to do wrong when the country's policy calls for such an action.

We recall how leading officials condemned and punished the lack of wholehearted support which they professed to find among some Americans of non-British origin, as well as among pacifists and socialists. It could be assumed that these groups had fulfilled the responsibilities laid upon them by the state, but not with joy and enthusiasm. In this country, there were Americans of German or Austrian origin who had close relatives in the enemy camps and who could not perform their duties or offer their sacrifices without suffering deep pain and anguish. Here also were pacifists who regarded all war as a relic of barbarism, people whose religious convictions branded all military conflicts as sin. Here were socialists whose commitment to the materialistic interpretation of history which they had openly advocated for about two generations obliged them to view the war as a manifestation of commercial rivalry with its consequences. That these people were off the track is quite another matter. When these groups of citizens brought their "coin" and unstintingly discharged their civic duties, it should have been conceded that their obligation to the government had been fulfilled. The state had the right to require of them the same degree of physical or material co-operation required of other citizens. It had no right, however, to demand an accounting of their inner convictions while they were fulfilling their other obligations without stint.

And if a government finds itself constrained to adopt coercive measures in order to regulate or control thought and conscience, it is clearly demanding of human beings an accounting not due to the state but rather to God.

[3] Stephen Decatur (1779–1820) was an American naval officer. Decatur's complete toast, given at a dinner in Norfolk, Virginia, in April, 1816, to celebrate victory over the Barbary pirates, was: "Our country: in her intercourse with foreign nations, may she always be in the right; but our country, right or wrong!"

The officially sponsored Americanization drive today confronts one with a similar phenomenon. In a speech to the jury in the case of *U. S. v Fontant*, Judge Charles Fremont Amidon of North Dakota commented that the accused had failed "to build up an American soul within himself." The inclination of the defendant's heart was adjudicated in court, an institution which ordinarily assumes jurisdiction only where overt action is involved. This episode attracted attention, not because it marked a departure from customary legal procedure, but because the judge's remark helped convict the accused in a verdict commanding widespread approval.

An inevitable question arises: What is an "American" soul? Does it differ in nature from others — souls subject to other laws? Does the Lord recognize American, Norwegian, Belgian, or Italian souls? Building an American one cannot mean building a devout spirit, since this may also be done outside of America. Nor can it mean a conscientious or honorable soul, since such a one is independent of geography — not even humble, compassionate, or patient — and since nothing of the kind can be built in this country which cannot also be built in Canada, Mexico, or Uruguay.

The only remaining supposition is that a person endowed with an American soul is one who loves everything American with all his strength, reason, and being. In this context, the term "American" denotes more than the geographic concept; it also embraces American literature, history, the country's great men, and its ideals. And one must not cultivate an attachment to any other country's history, culture, or literature. For according to the standard of loyalty dictated by current American foreign policy, love of any other country's music, literature, architecture, or natural setting constitutes divided allegiance, and bears witness to an incomplete national spirit.

However, none of these suppositions apply to Americans of British ancestry. The British-American soul has not yet become an object of official or juridical concern.

To require the poor immigrant who arrives here unfamiliar with the English language, excluded from American circles, and destined for the most exhausting daily toil, to build a new inner life is an unreasonable demand. Moreover, the first goal is to destroy the soul he came with.

In order to liquidate this speck of moral force that the immigrant may have brought over here, someone has concocted a plan to isolate him from foreign influences by admonishing him to abandon his native tongue, the only language capable of providing him with cultural nourishment. This is a spiritual blockade calculated to starve his foreign soul. The command that he must build in himself a new soul must be accompanied by an authorized blueprint for this different inner spirit, one prepared in all details by salaried government functionaries in Washington. Whether this edict should evoke tears or laughter is a good question; it is both very stupid and terribly cruel.

The generally accepted Americanization program is patterned on a kind of religious evangelism. In America, we have always been more rigid theologically than sociologically. Americanization must proceed through the same stages as salvation — in these steps:

(1) As a sinner, the immigrant must acknowledge his own shame and misery, that is to say, the dismal situation under which he lived in the old country and the disgrace of having come from another land. He must be appropriately humbled by these realities.

(2) A conversion is expected. One resolves that he will immediately divest himself of the old Adam, which is his homeland's language, history, memories, feelings of kinship, and all that his heart cherishes. He must take on new attributes which are comprehensively blueprinted by the national Americanization Bureau with subordinate branches in the various states.

(3) The process of sanctification consists of an all-out effort to hate (or ignore) what one previously loved or found pleasurable, together with a concomitant effort to love what the authorities command one to love. Thereby one becomes captive to the obedience of faith so that one knows nothing of upright conduct or good citizenship except what one hears and reads in English, and in that language alone.

The only flaw in these steps is that after his forced transformation the immigrant should be "saved," that is, made happy, which manifestly he is not. Nor is he promised happiness. But we understand that the transformation must be accomplished, forcibly if necessary, so that the immigrant's fellow citizens of British origin may similarly be saved.

Americans of British origin are not happy now. Judge Amidon was alarmed that there are still many immigrants who in their hearts nourish love for people other than those who were here before them. And official as well as semiofficial governmental actions indicate that a great and impending danger threatens the older Americans because some immigrants are laggard in committing their affections solely to the Americans who were here before them and who, not long before, were immigrants themselves. These early comers need the undivided love of the later arrivals in order to get along.

When an immigrant arrived in Eau Claire years ago, he was asked about his willingness and capacity to carry boards and planks or to cut timber in the woods. Nothing was demanded with respect to his state of mind while he carried planks or cut timber. The employer did not require his laborers to do these tasks with shouts of exaltation and enthusiasm. He asked only that planks be carried. Nor did he require the employee to love him because he paid an honest wage for an honest day's work, but he might, nevertheless, win the employee's affection if he was honorable and considerate. He could not have beaten or starved his workers into loving him.

The slogan that has been most emphasized in recent years is "one hundred per cent Americanism." It ought to signify a completely harmonious relationship with the state, an unstinting fulfillment of one's civic responsibilities. It clearly means that one renders to Caesar *all* that is Caesar's. However, these words denote not only citizenship, but citizenship plus everything American.

In public policy, which in a special way concerns the state, there are presently two sharply conflicting points of view with respect to what is American. The two leading and most responsible exponents of the country's foreign policy — President Woodrow Wilson and Senator Henry Cabot Lodge — stand opposed to one another. Surely both are one hundred percent Americans; they are acknowledged as such even by their adversaries. Thus a person's views on public affairs cannot define his relationship to the state. If the argument about "Americanism" means fidelity to American life and traditions, the problem becomes even more complex, since it is impossible to separate American culture from what has been imported.

The slogan has appeared because we have among us many immigrant citizens who communicate with one another in foreign languages and maintain their own churches, societies, and newspapers, thus creating a foreign and therefore un-American impression. Hence those who do not understand these languages regard the campaign to eliminate immigrant institutions as an important step in Americanization.

It should not be difficult to perceive that a newspaper owned, published, and edited by American citizens in their own and the country's interests is actually an American newspaper, regardless of the language of publication. Nor should it be difficult to understand that a journal published in English but owned by a British newspaper syndicate may be a foreign paper even if the language is that of the United States. A language is, of course, only outward attire.

If a ban on foreign language should deprive the immigrant of his churches, newspapers, and societies, then his morale, knowledge, and education, together with his zest for work and his efficiency, would sink far below present levels. He would become a less useful, less contented citizen, and we would run the risk of losing the best and most "American" traits in his mentality, the traits that could not tolerate coercion.

From the country's standpoint this development could hardly be for the best. Maintaining a labor force imbued with a desire to work is one of our most serious problems. The willingness of old-stock Americans to work does not rank at one hundred percent, notwithstanding the resolutions they adopt.

There is a danger in setting up either the state or the nationality concept as an object of worship. When the emperors of Rome set themselves up as worthy of worship and permitted their "golden images to stand as gods on the capitol," the Roman empire moved toward its fall.

Before the recent war, the Germans had established a virtual worship of Germanness. They had become exceedingly powerful and regarded themselves as more capable and better than other nations and hence also called upon to dominate them. We note, too, our tendency to use the word "American" as synonymous with something perfect — an ideal to emulate.

To love anything outside America's boundaries is almost regarded as disloyal. If one loves the literature, music, or natural setting of his homeland or of another country, he is not a one hundred percent American. Nor should he speak foreign languages, not even his mother tongue. President Theodore Roosevelt called this a desire "to serve two masters."

Roosevelt's phrase has a religious connotation, indicating that the civil realm has been set up for worship. "Thou shalt have no other Gods." . . . Being an American signifies only birth in America of American parents, just as birth in Norway of Norse parents makes one a Norwegian. It is merely a matter of geography and ancestry. One can be an extremely incompetent or wicked human being and at the same time be either an American or a Norwegian. If one reaches the point where he regards himself or his nationality as the embodiment of an ideal, his development is then complete; a natural consequence is that further growth ceases, and he seeks instead to shape others in his own image.

This is a demand for dominion over souls. They are to be reduced or enlarged as dictated by an American norm. Their spiritual life is to be standardized by force, even if this process cripples it.

A state has absolutely no right to interfere with such concerns of the heart as, for example, love of parents and kin or attachment to one's childhood home. Nor can it interfere with one's cultural tastes or preferences within its domain, when these in no way conflict with the governing body's legitimate interests. One is permitted, for example, enthusiasm for Greek history, one can regard Shakespeare as a greater poet than any American, one can perceive Alexander, Hannibal, Caesar, or Napoleon as greater generals than Pershing[4] without being imprisoned. And one may prefer Norwegian, Swedish, or Hungarian folk music to our own jazz. There are astronomers in our country more interested in Jupiter's moons than in the Monroe Doctrine, but they are not for that reason deported.

The nation must avoid enacting legislation which affects concerns of the heart and mind. A man may not be punished for being angry so long as his anger harms no one else. He may not even be convicted of villainy in his heart if he commits no villainous act. The state can never successfully judge souls. The Lord has reserved jurisdiction in that area. We owe the state no accounting of the inclinations of our hearts — only of our actions.

"Render unto Caesar what is Caesar's." Christ did not say "the Roman state." Caesar represented government, the ruling and reigning authority. Nor did Christ say "what Caesar demands." One owed

---

[4] John J. Pershing (1860–1948) was the American commanding general in Europe in World War I.

governments what was due them — what they had the right to demand — nothing more.

The coin of the realm was and is a material asset. Government has the right to demand a great deal. A citizen is obliged to sacrifice all his property if this is required. The state's jurisdiction over material goods is unlimited. Without a central authority, material values would scarcely exist. What we possess materially derives from the protection of the state.

Our constitution specifies what the government may demand of its citizens, the premise being that public officials will stay within its bounds. And the authority conferred by the constitution is linked to the will of the people as this finds expression in our legislative assemblies. Citizens are obligated to provide all that the governmental machine needs in order to operate, and we also are obligated to clear away every impediment to its operation. One cannot take his responsibilities toward the state too seriously; usually they are not taken seriously enough.

The worst evils currently hampering government are disrespect for law, dishonesty, private economic interests seeking to exploit government for their own advantage, incompetence, and carelessness in electing men to public office. However, this situation is unrelated to national background or to language. Public corruption is of ancient vintage, and it is attributable neither to immigration nor to the immigrant's slowness in abandoning his mother tongue.

The cancer of corruption came from the higher and most influential circles of society and has spread to the lower ranks. This is not the place to point an accusing finger at any class or national group. We are all more or less responsible for our governmental machinery, and we should offer the Publican's prayer, even if a pharisaical Plymouth Rock politician stands at the nation's high altar and thanks God that he is not like one of these "hyphenates," from whom nearly all evil comes.

But the governmental machine cannot be purified and improved if it is placed on an altar for worship. Then all that would remain for us would be to idolize it and to sacrifice to it. No one should be more alert with respect to what is owed the state than we who are immigrants. We entered willingly into a contract with this nation, and if we do not know what we agreed to, this lack of knowledge is our own fault. We must create the most alert watch possible to guard against the disruptive tendencies that have spread through society in our time. We are obligated to become thoroughly familiar with our government and its constitution. Doing this is rendering to Caesar what is Caesar's.

And if we do this, the state is obligated not to block our opportunity to give God what is God's. The government should allow us — insofar as we find it practical — to seek nourishment for our soul through our mother tongue, the instrument the Lord gave us. The Lord endowed the human being with a soul. It is not to be administered by the state.

XII

Waldemar Theodore Ager
1869–1941

by Kenneth Smemo

W ALDEMAR AGER once remarked that he was eternally grateful for having been blessed with a good memory, an appetite for work, and little need for sleep. His career among his Norwegian countrymen in America gives ample testimony to the truth of this statement, as he labored for over half a century in behalf of a multitude of idealistic causes whose common denominator was *norskdom* (Norwegianness) in America — its past, its present, and its future. His crusade over a long and active lifetime was truly a labor of love, for his material rewards were scant, barely providing for himself and his large family, as he kept his little publishing enterprise going from one debt-ridden week to the next.

He loved Norway, he loved the best of her cultural riches which he worked to transplant firmly into the Norwegian community in America, and he loved his immigrant group in this land, as it adjusted itself, often painfully and, in Ager's view, sometimes foolishly, to its new American environment. His loves were passionate and sincere, although not uncritical, and they were often unrequited. In his later years, he was honored by his fellow immigrants and their descendants, when, ironically, his most ardent hopes and dreams had shown themselves to be beyond fulfillment. Only now, in the latter part of the twentieth century, is the ultimate wisdom of his message and his vision coming to be acknowledged by many among the descendants of Norwegian and other immigrant groups who question the validity and the value of the melting pot ideal.

Ager defended "ethnicity" before the word was invented; he argued the case for "cultural pluralism" in America long before it was either in vogue or semantically referred to in this way. Much of what he wrote in the early decades of this century has a surprisingly contemporary ring to it, which suggests that he was *more* than just an apologist for a small group of Norwegian immigrants in a time which is long past and whose condition, then and since, should be of interest only to the historian or the Norwegian-American antiquarian.

His tireless efforts in behalf of The Norwegian Society, of which he was one of the founding spirits in 1903, typify his work for the retention of *norskdom* in America. Over the years, he served as secretary and as treasurer for the organization, and some of his best essays in defense of Norwegianness appeared in the pages of the Society's quarterly journal, *Kvartalskrift*, which he edited throughout the period of its existence from 1905 through 1922. The high quality of the material that appeared in this magazine and, indeed, the very fact that the small publication saw the light of day, one issue after the other, were almost solely due to Ager's dedication and concern. And the preserved body of essays, articles, and short fictional pieces which the issues of *Kvartalskrift* contain well represents the tireless efforts of Ager and a small group of Norwegian Americans of like thought, who fought for retention of ethnicity in the face of relentless Americanization and homogenization of America's immigrant strains.

Waldemar Ager was born in 1869 in Fredrikstad, along the east coast of the Oslofjord, and grew up in nearby Gressvik. His father had a problem with alcoholism, and had failed in attempting to operate a country store. He had left for America promising to send for his wife and three small children. There followed some years of utter poverty in Kristiania, during which young Waldemar became active in a Christian youth temperance group. After a time, the mother's family scraped together funds to send her and the children to Chicago to find the father. Ager's formal education in Norway ended with the common school, but he was already an avid and voracious reader at an early age — as he reported later — and he remained so all his life.

Arriving in Chicago at the age of sixteen, Waldemar became an errand boy and apprentice typesetter in *Norden's* newspaper office, where he learned not only the printer's trade but gained journalistic writing experience as well. Here, too, he joined a Norwegian temperance lodge and soon was made editor of the group's little publication. In 1892, when he was twenty-three, he moved to Eau Claire, Wisconsin, where he had accepted a job as typesetter and business manager for a recently begun Norwegian-language temperance weekly, *Reform*. Upon the sudden death of its editor, Ager succeeded him in 1903. From then until his death from cancer in 1941, he edited, wrote, and traveled extensively for *Reform*, managed its finances and book-publication activities, and ultimately became owner of the enterprise.

Reform was the major vehicle for agitation and popularization of his causes among Norwegians in America, and it was regarded by Ager's contemporaries as a well-edited, sprightly, witty, and highly personal journal. It made its editor's name a well-known and often controversial one, as he left his readers with no doubts as to his positions on contemporary issues and controversies in the Norwegian-American subculture. Prominent among his efforts toward reform were his dedication to abstinence from alcohol and to cultural preservation among his people. The popularity of his paper over the decades, among those who agreed with him and those who did not, was no doubt sustained by virtue of his engaging journalistic style, which showed a keen and shrewd mind combined with compassion and good humor. Never the grim, thundering user of bombast, Ager tempered his contentions with wit and irony, his arguments with a folkwise bubbling good humor, and his pleas with warmth and love of his fellowman. During the thirty-eight years of his editorship, as one contemporary put it, *"Reform* was Ager and Ager was *Reform."* He avidly encouraged literary creativity, rooted in the experiences of the Norwegians in America, and he devoted a good deal of space in his paper to literary reviews and criticism. He made it possible for dozens of Norwegian-language writers to get their work into print through his book-publishing activities, although rarely at a profit to the firm.

Aside from the strenuous and often precarious task of keeping the paper and publishing house going, he was a man of apparently inexhaustible energy, who worked actively in dozens of Norwegian-American projects, promotions, and organizations. He traveled widely about the Midwest speaking and founding Norwegian Good Templar lodges, temperance societies, Norwegian ski clubs, and lodges of the Sons of Norway and the Scandinavian-American Fraternity. Aside from his work for The Norwegian Society, he was a founder and working member of the Norsk-Danske Presseforening (The Norwegian-Danish Press Association), Avholdskongressen (The Abstinence Congress), Nordmanns-Forbundet (League of Norsemen), the Norwegian-American Historical Association, the Wisconsin Prohibition Party, the *bygdelag* movement, and the Rølvaag-inspired preservationist group called For Fædrearven. He organized and headed the Wisconsin exhibit at the Norwegian exposition to commemorate the centennial of the Eidsvoll Constitution in Kristiania in 1914. He contributed a stream of articles, literary criticisms, and short stories regularly to dozens of Norwegian publications in America and in Norway, including *Smaalenslagets aarbog* (of which he was editor), *Symra* (Decorah, Iowa), *Jul i Vesterheimen* (Minneapolis), *Nordmanns-Forbundet* (Kristiania) and *Menneskevennen* (the journal of the Norwegian national abstinence society, Kristiania), as well as *Kvartalskrift*.

He became a popular public speaker who was much in demand throughout Norwegian America, as well as in Norway, where he went on lecture tours three times. His themes were usually some aspect of Norwegianness, temperance, or the need for the retention of culture. His contemporaries found him warm, witty, gently ironic, and thoroughly engaging; his platform appearances were as ubiquitous as was his little newspaper *Reform* among his people in America. He may have delivered as many as a thousand speeches throughout his lifetime, at all manner of occasions, from one American coast to the other.

Furthermore, Ager found the time and the inspiration to write six novels and eight volumes of short stories, as well as occasional poetry. Most of his creative writing was done at night when his wife and nine children were asleep and the house was quiet. A short man of slight build, he remained a dynamo of energy and activity until his rather sudden death in 1941 at the age of seventy-two.

It was his lot to agitate passionately over a lifetime for, essentially, three idealistic causes — all doomed to eventual failure. He advocated total abstinence and the prohibition of alcoholic beverages through public enlightenment as well as by law, through Norwegian-constituted societies and organizations which used the Norwegian language in their agitation. Second, he sought the retention of a permanent Norwegian subculture in America, a bilingual society based on the culture and traditions of the Norwegian people, tempered, however, by America's physical and social setting, and therefore peculiarly Norwegian-American, no longer wholly Norwegian nor wholly Anglo-American. And third, he steadfastly encouraged all types of artistic activity within this hybrid culture, but especially literary creativity which would rely on the mother tongue and be drawn from the life experiences of the ethnic group in its new-world setting. A bridge between the two cultures must be maintained, he wrote, and "in reality it is the language — the Norwegian language — which is the bridge. When the language no longer carries, then there is no bridge."

Throughout his life, Ager promoted creative writing and publication among Norwegian Americans. He wrung his hands in the face of the apathy with which this writing was often received by Norwegians in this country, and he was driven to despair by the almost total rejection of it by the literary establishment in Norway. He earned respect among many of his peers for the quality of his literary criticism, as he sought to raise the level of Norwegian-American literature and to urge its public acceptance and support. Like his contemporaries and close personal friends, Ole E. Rølvaag and Simon Johnson, he aided the cause by writing creatively himself, thereby helping to build a body of Norwegian-American *belles-lettres* of high quality.

His first short novel and the collections of short pieces published in his early years can be quite easily dismissed as naive, amateurish temperance propaganda. A book of short stories published in 1908, however, *Hverdagsfolk* (Everyday People) shows Ager moving away from temperance didacticism, using his keen eye for observation and his storytelling abilities to greater effect as he drew small, poignant vignettes of everyday people in his contemporary immigrant society. From this time on, he dealt largely with realistic situations in his fiction, and Ager the mature social critic ultimately emerges with an engaging, individualistic narrative style, a liberal use of satire and irony, and an overall concern for the broader human and social problems of his group.

He became the first Norwegian-American writer to be accepted for publication in Norway when Aschehoug published *Kristus for Pilatus* (Christ Before Pilate) in 1910, entitled *Presten Conrad Walther Welde* in the Norwegian edition. In that year, he was given the literary award of The Norwegian Society for this novel. The book was generally well received by critics in Norway, but Norwegian interest in their countrymen in America was still not very great compared to what it would be several decades later. No Norwegian publisher again took a chance on a Norwegian-American novel until *I de dage*, the first volume of Rølvaag's *Giants in the Earth*, was brought out in Oslo in 1924. Aschehoug ultimately published two more of Ager's novels set in Norwegian America, *Gamlelandets sønner* (Sons of the Old Country, 1926) and *Hundeøine* (1929), translated as *I Sit Alone*. His fiction, like his articles and essays, bore the urgent warning to his fellow immigrants that to deny and reject their Norwegian heritage, for themselves and for their descendants, would leave them in a spiritual and cultural void, with only a superficial Americanization and the gathering of material goods as their sole reasons for existence in this land.

During World War I and into the decade of the twenties, the Norwegian champions of preserving their national culture energetically continued to advance their cause, its legitimacy and its importance, in the face of the intense pressures for abandoning "hyphenism" and for the "100 per cent Americanism" of that period. Well-known and respected figures like Ole E. Rølvaag, Simon Johnson, and Jon Norstog stood, like Ager, as bulwarks against the rapidly encroaching Americanization of their people. When the door to further immigration from the fatherland began to be closed in 1921, the era of Norwegian cultural retention was clearly ending.

With growing disappointment, Ager watched the failures of his three great crusades. National prohibition had proved clearly unworkable and the temperance movement had been largely repudiated. Permanent retention of the Norwegian language and culture was doomed, and there were but few writers left in the old tradition — and they were writing for an aging and rapidly diminishing audience. By the 1930s, the world he had known so well and in which he played such an active role was disintegrating around him, and he felt himself an embittered anachronism left over from another day, another era, a feeling which is reflected in his last novel, *Hundeøine*. But he persevered; he continued to write, to agitate, to speak to whoever would listen. Until the day he died, *Reform* came out every week, but for an ever-shrinking subscription list.

Ager's writings, fictional, editorial, and philosophical, remain his legacy to the present and the future. They not only constitute a lode for historians who seek to better understand Norwegian life in America in its cultural heyday and after, but they also establish that Ager's cogent pleas for ethnic retention, language preservation, and recognition of the social and psychological importance of cultural pluralism in America are still worthy of study and consideration.